AN INTRODUCTION TO THE STUDY OF HISTORY

John A. Maxwell
Sandra Barney
Mary Heironimus
Department of History
West Virginia University

KENDALL/HUNT PUBLISHING COMPANY
2460 Kerper Boulevard P.O. Box 539 Dubuque, Iowa 52004-0539

This edition has been printed directly from camera-ready copy.

Copyright © 1993 by Kendall/Hunt Publishing Company

ISBN 0-8403-8707-5

All rights reserved. No part of this publication may be reproduced, stored in a retrieval system, or transmitted, in any form or by any means, electronic, mechanical, photocopying, recording, or otherwise, without the prior written permission of the copyright owner.

Printed in the United States of America.
10 9 8 7 6 5 4 3 2 1

TABLE OF CONTENTS

Preface i

Introduction iii

Chapter 1 - What Is History? 1
    What Is History? 1
    Role Of Facts 1
    Interpretation 2
    Philosophy Of History 6
    What Is Not History? 8
    Television Dramas And Non-Histories 9
    Subjectivity 12
    Why Study History? 13
    History's Place In A Liberal Arts Education 15
    History - Science Or Not? 18
    Careers For History Majors 19
    Conclusion 21
    Endnotes 22
    Bibliography 25

Chapter 2 - Using The Library 27
    Introduction 27
    Reference Room 27
    Examples 30
    The Card Catalog 30
    Using The Card Catalog 35
    Types Of Cards In The Card Catalog 36
    Call Numbers 37

Initial Research	38
Journal Research	39
Historical Indices	40
Newspaper Research	42
Other Primary Sources	43
Government Documents	44
Other Resource Tools	45
Conclusion	46

Chapter 3 - Writing For History Classes 47

  Part 1 - Writing A Research Paper 47
Introduction	47
Reading The Documents You Have Gathered	47
Taking Research Notes	48
Writing A Thesis Statement	52
Outlining	53
Writing Aids	57
Introductions And Conclusions	57
The Body Of The Paper	58
Twelve Basic Rules For Good Writing	60
Using Other's Work: Do's and Don'ts	62
Manuals Of Style	63
Footnotes And Endnotes	64
Bibliography	65
Choosing A Title	66
First Drafts	66

  Part 2 - Taking Notes In Class And
               Preparing For Examinations 68
Taking Notes In Class	68
Writing In Class Assignments	68
Essay Examinations	69
Short Answer And Identifications	70

      Miscellaneous Test Taking Suggestions 71
      Conclusion 71
      Endnotes 72

Chapter 4 - Basic Bibliography 73

Appendix A - Types Of History 91

Appendix B - Research Guides 93

Appendix C - Historical Societies And Organizations . . . 96

Index 99

PREFACE

This volume is a result of numerous discussions within a typical Department of History about what students know and need to know in studying history at the introductory survey level. It is also the result of the three authors' long discussions with many faculty members and teaching assistants about what they would find most useful in an introduction to history for all of the surveys.

Mary Heironimus bore primary responsibility for the first chapter on what history is and is not; she also composed the bibliography, which includes recommendations of many faculty members. Sandra Barney carried the burden for the two chapters on how to use the library and how to write a history paper and prepare for exams.

Particularly generous with their time and suggestions were Professors Jack Hammersmith, Mary Lou Lustig, Steven McCluskey and John Super of the West Virginia University Department of History. Dawn Miller of the *Charleston Gazette* made many helpful recommendations on style and organization. Myra Lowe, Reference Librarian at the West Virginia University Wise Library, gave good professional advice on using the resources of a university library and in addressing students' problems. Professor Barbara Howe, former chair, National Council on Public History, authored *Careers for Students of History* (1989) which provided much information on the job market for history majors. Deirdre DeGolia gave invaluable help in formatting and preparing the book for publication.

This volume also resulted from the participation of faculty members at our university in the Holmes Group Consortium's consideration of means to improve the preparation of teachers. The Claude Worthington Benedum Foundation supported the Holmes project at West Virginia University and made available funds for two of the authors to complete this work. Professor Perry D. Phillips and Assistant Dean Katherine C. Lovell of the College of Human Resources and Education at West Virginia University encouraged this project at every stage.

Profits realized from the sale of this volume will accrue to the Rebecca Donnally and Henry Everett Thornburg Scholarship Fund which will enable graduate students in history at West Virginia University to research their doctoral dissertations.

INTRODUCTION

A student beginning history courses at the college level is faced with many problems which this volume hopes to address. Many of the fine books about the discipline of history are written for the advanced student with considerable experience in many facets of the historian's craft. This book was written with the beginner in mind and thus seeks to assist this person in an introductory discussion of questions that arise. What is history? How do you find and use the resources of a college library for papers and exams? What is learned from a card catalogue or an on-line terminal? How do you take notes for a paper? How does an outline help in writing a paper or taking an exam? What are some introductory works in the field that might get a student started in finding materials?

One professor assigns different texts for students to compare in order that his students become sensitized to the variety of approaches to history. This historian teaches them that in order to focus and to explore some aspects of history, a conscious decision must be made on what to eliminate from consideration. Thus a society may be examined with greater concentration if many political developments are left to others, for example.

This project required similar decisions on exclusions. This is not a style manual, although very basic advice is given on common mistakes made in writing, and correct forms for bibliographies and footnotes or endnotes are presented. This is not a history of history nor of the philosophies of history. Examples are given, however, of philosophies of history as well as examples of historians' conflicts over interpretations of historical developments.

Finally, this book was designed as an aid for students to get into the study of history for the very first time, while offering something to students who are more experienced but are facing their first term papers or essay exams. For faculty, it was designed to cover some of the details that need to be presented as a foundation for their further development of ideas and assignments that go beyond the range of this book.

CHAPTER 1

WHAT IS HISTORY?

WHAT IS HISTORY?

History is both the past itself and our best obtainable account of what people did and how they lived. History is useful when people try to answer some of the fundamental, recurring questions of human existence. Who are we? Where did we come from? Where are we going? The search for answers to these common questions begins with a study of the past, because the past may help explain the present. Understanding the present, in turn, gives us some keys to make decisions for the future.

Thoughtful people have always wrestled with these questions. The study of history helps people find a few of their own answers and offers clues to why things are as they are.

ROLE OF FACTS

Facts are the building blocks of history. Accurate facts about past peoples, places, and events serve as mileposts in the human story. They are essential to our understanding of historical change. Historians use facts as trial lawyers use evidence; both search for their facts as close to the original time, place, person, or subject as they can.

They find historical facts in documents, archives, excavation sites, voting records, photographs, newspapers, letters, diaries, trial records, and oral interviews to name a few places. Not all facts are equally valuable or trustworthy. From the start, historians must sort through all the facts they can gather. They hunt for what they need and what they can trust. By carefully studying their sources and facts, they try to reconstruct events and add to our knowledge of what came before us.

Professional historians often write of events, people, and places about which they have a particular interest. To be accurate, this work requires detailed amounts of research. But not all written histories are tales of remote events told long after the fact, nor are the records always reported by historians.

Contemporary writers may record their experiences from within an event, as a participant. British Prime Minister Winston Churchill (1874-1965) described his experiences in his work, *The Second World War*. Many years before Churchill, Thucydides (455?-399? B.C.) wrote *The History of the Peloponnesian War*. A more recent observer of events, Theodore White (1915-1986) wrote *The Making of a President 1960*.

Contemporary historians give us much raw data and eye-witness material in their work.[1] Their accounts may resonate with an immediacy that makes exciting reading, but be careful. Contemporary accounts may be exciting; they may also be wrong, or give only one side of the story. American historian Barbara Tuchman (1918-1989), in her book *A Distant Mirror*, recalled a story told by the medieval chronicler, Jean Froissart (1337-1410) about the French Sire Enguerrand de Coucy in 1374. De Coucy disguised himself, Froissart wrote, abandoned his personal mercenary army in the field at Alsace, and fled. Returning to Paris, he told the king that his soldiers had refused to move forward and had plotted to sell him to the enemy. "The fact that nothing of the kind ever happened illustrates the problem of medieval records," Tuchman wrote.[2] It illustrates similar problems in records from other eras as well.

INTERPRETATION

Facts alone are not history. They must be interpreted – lined up and logically connected to explain past events and human conditions.

The interpreter of history carefully examines the facts of an event or of a person's life and actions. The historian must strive not to diminish or embellish the facts, but to be certain they are as accurate as possible.

The historian first asks, "What happened?" Having accumulated available information on the subject at hand, and judged that the facts are correct, the interpreter begins the task of determining "how it really was."

When interpreting, historians may consider such influences as a nation's form of, or lack of, government; climate; available food and water; the wisdom or folly of it's leaders and enemies; religious beliefs and social customs. By placing the facts within the broader context of peoples, times, and places, more useful understanding of the past emerges.

History may have recurring similarities and questions, but it is never static. It moves constantly in the stream of peoples and human events, molding and shaping them and being molded and shaped by them. In time, another historian will examine some or many past interpretations and will rethink and rewrite them in light of new understanding, different attitudes, or with newly available information.

Let us put all these ideas into a concrete example. Our fact is familiar. Christopher Columbus discovered America in 1492. Actually, he first discovered an island that he called "San Salvador" and then another island that he named "Hispaniola." Of this discovery, the historian, Samuel Eliot Morison (1887-1976), wryly noted:

> America was discovered accidentally by a great seaman who was looking for something else; when discovered it was not wanted; and most of the exploration for the next fifty years was done in the hope of getting through or around it. America was named after a man who discovered no part of the New World. History is like that, very chancy.[3]

Columbus recorded his discovery from his point of view – the only one he had. In 1892, bibliographer Paul Leicester Ford (1865-1902) translated Columbus' written accounts into English. According to Ford's translation, Columbus wrote:

> I discovered many islands, thickly peopled, of which I took possession without resistance in the name of our most illustrious Monarch. We kidnapped several natives,...taught them the rudiments of our language,...and to introduce us to other Indians as, "Come, come and look upon beings of a celestial race."[4]

As far as we know, the Arawaks Columbus met on the islands left no record of the meeting, or of what he said.

In the 1800s, American and European historians – the major interpreters – with the advantage of hindsight, agreed that Columbus' discovery was a great boon and a major achievement of Western Civilization. Europeans established colonies in the New World and some became rich from the newly-found resources and the expanded trade.

Generations of students have learned these facts of Columbus' discovery. The settlers, coming from "civilized" countries, believed that they had a God-given right to bring the benefits of their civilization to this "howling wilderness." They were called to save the "heathens" whom they found here, do away with their superstitions, and convert the natives to the settlers' religion. Columbus became a hero; we celebrate the date of his landing as a national holiday.

However, as the 500th anniversary of Columbus' arrival approached, a lively discussion erupted again as other scholars began to reinterpret these same facts. Instead of a "discovery," perhaps what Columbus really did was to be the first of an on-going invasion of the two continents by Europeans. Using these viewpoints and many more, present-day historians reevaluated Columbus himself, the peoples he found here, and the impact on them of the sudden appearance of white, European males from more politically and economically developed societies. Present-day historian Garry Wills concluded:

> The old view was that Columbus did something almost superhuman, so he had to have superhuman qualities to explain this marvel. The real truth – and no wonder people have been avoiding it for so long – is that Columbus in himself is rather a bore. No genius, no villain, he was a better courtier than administrator, a better navigator than captain, a man whose recorded thought was neither deep nor original....He was certainly persistent and stubborn in sticking to [his expedition] – and some have tried to make him a giant at least in his "obsession," for good or ill.[5]

Some historians have also taken a different point of view about the continents' people. Instead of standing on the eastern shore with Columbus, looking in at a forest full of "savages," they stand in the forest with the original inhabitants and see the invading white hordes from Europe, bringing deadly disease, hatred, deprivation and conquest. These people, too, have a history.

What was the impact of discovery upon the original peoples of the Americas? Estimates of pre-Columbian populations vary widely. One for Hispaniola estimates a population of just under eight million people in 1496. By 1518 one Spanish survey numbered the precipitously-declining population at under 100,000 persons. The most detailed census available suggests that 8 million people were reduced to a mere 28,000 in just over 20 years. More than 99 percent of the population died within a single generation.[6]

As explorers moved onto the continents, they continued to

interact with existing populations, weakening them with disease, warfare, and abuse. Modern demographic research suggests the Aztec Empire in Mexico contained approximately 25.2 million people before Hernando Cortés arrived in 1519. By 1585 the number was reduced to 1.9 million.[7] The impact of European conquest was devastating. Historians now confront these terrible results for the original peoples. Their revised historical accounts of "discovery" and exploration of the New World reflect that understanding.

These recent historians do not remake history. They start with essentially the same facts previous historians had. However, they also look for information in new places in order to answer new questions shaped by changing values, insights, and new sensitivities of the present-day. In the future, facts will be assembled once more from the vantage point of another time, experience, and understanding, and perhaps other interpretations will emerge. In history, there is no such thing as the last word.

PHILOSOPHY OF HISTORY

Throughout time, historians have tried to find one theory that explains human history. Such a theory is called a philosophy of history. Consider this example: during Europe's Industrial Revolution, young Karl Marx (1818-1883) of Germany attempted to explain change in human history. His ideas proved to be revolutionary. "History," according to Marx, "is a contest among individuals, groups, classes, and states, for food, fuel, materials, and economic power."[8]

Beginning with ancient times, Marx analyzed succeeding epochs by asking: How was wealth produced and who owned the means of production?

In agricultural societies, people who controlled land and crops held wealth and power. During the Industrial Revolution, factory owners controlled wealth and had power over masses of people dependent on factory work for a living. Marx decided that economic conditions produced ruling classes who in turn shaped human institutions to protect their interests.

Workers, "the proletariat," produced the goods. Mill, factory, and mine owners sold the goods and collected the wealth. Workers received little for their labor. They lived in poverty. They worked long hours at dangerous jobs. Marx predicted that the deplorable conditions would worsen and lead to a crisis.

He believed an army of the unemployed proletariat would rise in revolt against the capitalist classes. A revolutionary dictatorship of the proletariat would appear in the most highly industrialized countries and would strip the middle class of its industrial wealth. The workers would then form a classless society where everybody owned everything.

Marx's ideas inspired people for decades after his death. Desperate people saw it as a doctrine of hope for the future. Twentieth-century Communists in Russia, Asia, Cuba, Africa, and North and South America based their actions on their understanding of Marx's philosophy.

A great many people agree that Marx's conclusions were wrong. The growth of trade union organizations in the late nineteenth and early twentieth centuries led to better working and living conditions in the West. By using their right to vote, workers elected governments more responsive to their needs. Marx's revolution occurred not in the most industrialized nations, as he had predicted, but in the least developed ones such as Russia and China.

By the 1990's, Marx's influence had waned as Communist parties began to give up power. Yet his philosophy of history remains important. Without knowing Marx's economic interpretation of history, for example, it is impossible to understand the work of Marxist historians or to realize why Communism is attractive to struggling developing countries.

Vast, sweeping explanations for history come and go. For

example, an important theme in American history is the idea of progress – that each generation will have a better life than the previous one. Another example is from British historian George Macaulay Trevelyan (1876-1962) who compared societies with plants. They sprang from seeds in appropriate soil, grew to maturity under the right conditions, and died when conditions deteriorated. Like plants, cultures could adapt themselves and change to avoid decline. Trevelyan's thinking was consistent with the new Darwinian emphasis on evolution that emerged in the late nineteenth century.

The countless philosophies of history provide a vital field of study for advanced history students. Each philosophy is important but beyond the scope of this book.

WHAT IS NOT HISTORY?

Television, with its immediacy, drama, and instant replay, has forever changed the way we perceive our world and our past. "There are events," former NBC News chief Reuven Frank has observed, "which exist in the American mind and recollection primarily because of television."[9] After the reporters and commentators are done speaking, what remains for us is image – what we have seen on the television screen. This universal viewing of an event results in what one journalist has called a "meta-verdict," a shared judgment reached by many people in America and, very likely, by history.[10]

Consider this example. The television news coverage of the Vietnam War, in living color, accompanied millions of American dinnertimes throughout that long struggle. The official position was that the enemy, the Viet Cong and the North Vietnamese, were in retreat, that the war was winnable, and, indeed, that we were winning it.

During a cease-fire proclaimed for the 1968 Vietnamese Tet holiday, the Viet Cong in South Vietnam, with the aid of their North

Vietnamese counterparts, attacked an astonishing number of cities and strategic areas all across South Vietnam. The fighting was bloody and costly to both sides. The Viet Cong even penetrated onto the grounds of the United States Embassy and engaged the Marine guards there. Television recorded it all.

At the time, CBS news anchor Walter Cronkite was called "the most trusted man in America." In preparation for his nightly news broadcast, Cronkite previewed film of the Tet Offensive and exclaimed, "What the hell is going on? I though we were winning the war!"[11] When the public saw the same film, Cronkite's dismay resounded in homes and attitudes all across America. The image had been set.

Eventually United States forces regained the ground lost during the Tet Offensive. The Viet Cong forces were so severely reduced that the Tet Offensive became, in military terms, a large-scale defeat from which they never recovered.

None of that mattered to the American people who had seen the fighting and witnessed our forces besieged all over South Vietnam. The pictures, and especially those of Viet Cong fighters on the embassy grounds, provided the image from which Americans formed their meta-verdict. In the transcendent judgment of many Americans, the Tet Offensive was a defeat for United States forces.

The television camera makes possible "instant history" at a rate unthinkable in any previous time. No one yet has an answer to the question of how this will, in the future, affect the way we regard our past – and ourselves as a nation.

TELEVISION DRAMAS AND NON-HISTORIES

Rudyard Kipling once wrote:

Ah! what awaits the classic bent
And what the cultured word

*Against the undoctored incident
That actually occurred.*

Beside the Image History we see on the television nightly news, there are other kinds of Instant History. Television presents sensational dramas of past events for public entertainment. Popular novelists write exposé books. The film industry makes "tell-all" movies.

Producers of these forms of entertainment presume to offer to the public "new evidence of conspiracy," or "the shocking truth of what really happened that no one wants YOU to know," about historical events. They tout their stories as if only they had uncovered some heretofore hidden sources of alarming facts that all other investigators had failed to locate or had deliberately withheld.

These forms of entertainment "deal in elusive distinctions between fact and fantasy" and display "a disregard for the truth" notes historian Sean Wilentz.[12] Television's fictionalized dramas and the sensational film and literary exposés are careless with accepted facts, take liberties with history, and harm the people who accept their words as absolute truth. A difficult problem remains: artists must be assured "artistic license" in their creative work; historical dramas may be terribly wrong in the accuracy of historical fact.

We have already seen that there is always room for reinterpretation of facts in history. However, there are some central facts that are so much a part of history that rational thinkers do not question them: Abraham Lincoln was shot by John Wilkes Booth; William the Conqueror invaded England in 1066; Ancient Egyptians built the pyramids. A playwright or television producer, however, will probably add "human interest" items to the established facts. Thus conjectures about what went through William the Conquerer's mind as he approached the British coast will enliven a drama. Part of the historians job is to separate out what is fact from what is conjecture.

Consider an example of sensationalism from another era.

American history students are familiar with Emanual Leutze's painting, *Washington Crossing the Delaware*. Colonial America's top general stands nobly in the prow of a rowboat, holding his cloak shut against the cold, patriotic, and firm of purpose. The fact is undisputed: Washington crossed the Delaware.

Leutze's version is compelling, but unlikely. George Washington could not have stood in such a little boat without tipping it and pitching himself and his officers into the icy waters. Of course, it is difficult to look noble sitting in a rowboat surrounded by bedraggled soldiers, with your knees around your earlobes. The artist, a German man who had not been to America, had never seen the Delaware, but he did live near the Rhine River, which probably inspired him.

After seeing Leutze's version of the story, how many people retain it as their best obtainable account of what happened? When you think of Washington crossing the Delaware, what image comes to your mind? Examining where the story comes from – whether in a painting, TV show, book or movie – helps us determine how reliable the source is. We must develop the ability to distinguish between the sensationalized and the authentic.

Someone who carelessly or deliberately tampers with, shades, or omits central facts is working at cross-purposes with the historian. British historian George Kitson Clark states the problem clearly.

> The facts are the only part of history about which there is any degree of certainty; all interpretations, all reconstruction, is speculative, and if it does not respect the facts speculation is certainly worthless and may be deceptive.[13]

The goal of sensational television dramas and film and literary exposé entertainment is not to advance the sum total of knowledge. Its producers, directors, or writers may instead want to boost their ratings, make more money, or advance their own personal agendas. Therefore, the omission of relevant facts or the addition of titillating untruths is often an unfortunate by-product.

There is nothing wrong in writing a rousing good story about a historical period. But, unfortunately, even if the facts are wrong, people believe what they see, hear, and read and use half-truths and distortions to justify their hate, prejudice, and misunderstanding of the world.

Adolf Hitler once said that one should not tell little lies. Rather, it was important to tell big lies. People would believe them if they were told often enough. He proved his point. He convinced most of a nation that Jews were evil and the source of many of Germany's problems. If they removed Jews from German life, he told them, there were no limits to what the German people could achieve. Using mass communication and film, Hitler created propaganda and rewrote history to suit his own goals.

Education is for nothing if not to teach us to think critically for ourselves, examine the sources of our information, and be able to rely on our own ability to ascertain truth from lie. For our own personal well-being and for the future of the democratic society in which we live, nothing is more essential.

SUBJECTIVITY

Subjectivity means the sum total of attitudes that we all have. These attitudes are the result of external influences upon us, such as: when we were born, how and where we were raised, our education, and the impact of our environment on us as individuals. These factors help both to shape our values, likes, and dislikes and to determine those things which we consider important and interesting. Yet students of history must strive to be objective. Through education we become aware of our attitudes and are free to examine them.

There are events in history, which by their nature, make impartiality not only impossible but also reprehensible to the reader. The enslavement and exploitation of Africans by Arabs, Europeans, and Americans is one example. Another is Hitler's slaughter of six million Jewish people. Nonetheless, such developments must be examined with critical detachment. An accurate scholarly account does not make an historian a moral eunuch.

WHY STUDY HISTORY?

Well, if no historian ever has the last word, or all the facts and all authors are to some degree suspect, why study history?

Philosopher George Santayana (1863-1952) made the observation that "those who cannot remember the past are condemned to repeat it." Thus the mistakes of the past can be made again. But we must be careful, because we may learn the wrong lessons from history. For example, in order to avoid the mistakes of the 1930's, when leaders of the Western powers failed to stop Hitler, leaders of the United States involved this country in Vietnam in 1960. Had they learned the wrong lesson?

Many years ago, the Athenian Greek Thucydides was not even as optimistic as Santayana. Thucydides was convinced that humans would certainly encounter similar situations in the future, whether or not they learned from the past. Therefore, he wrote his account of the Peloponnesian War for

> ....those who want to understand clearly the events which happened in the past and which (human nature being what it is) will at some time or other and in much the same way be repeated in the future.[14]

Students of history develop judgment and a greater

understanding of themselves and the world around them. To write history, or to pioneer in science, one must be able to think critically and to challenge the truths of the past. For example, Galileo (1564-1642) was dissatisfied with the ancient assumption that the sun revolved around the earth. His observations and his constant, critical review of the facts led him to a different conclusion – that the planets move around the sun.

Paleontologist Stephen Jay Gould addressed this need to carefully evaluate facts when he observed:

> The results of history lie strewn around us, but we cannot, in principle, directly observe the processes that produced them....We must develop criteria for inferring the processes we cannot see from results that have been preserved.[15]

People who study history may also find some answers to the three questions at the beginning of this chapter. Who are we? Where did we come from? Where are we going? Every individual is a link in a chain that stretches back, two by two, through the millennia of human history. Students of this history gain at least a partial understanding of these people and their lives. With a little imagination and self-knowledge, history students may even empathize with the people they study.

To study history, one must understand that nothing happens in a vacuum, that the accidental and the irrational happen in human experience, and that not all problems have solutions.[16] History includes both the best and the worst that human beings are and do, and the loftiest and most ignoble of human thoughts and dreams. Our past conditions offer clues to future possibilities.[17] We use the inheritance from the past to understand the present and future – perhaps to avoid its gruesome errors and tragic turns. English historian E.H. Carr gave his reason for the study of history when he noted:

> History begins with the handing down of tradition; and tradition means the carrying of the habits and lessons of the past into the future. Records of the past begin to be kept for the benefit of future generations.[18]

HISTORY'S PLACE IN A LIBERAL ARTS EDUCATION

A liberal arts education is designed to provide general knowledge, to develop general intellectual abilities, such as reason and judgment, as opposed to more specific professional training. Most people get their liberal arts education as undergraduates at colleges and universities. American educator Ernest Boyer of the Carnegie Foundation for the Advancement of Teaching wrote that an undergraduate education enriches, and at best, transforms:

> Why else make it the prerequisite to professional study? Why else provide college for those who otherwise could be trained on the job or in a corporate classroom? It can only be because of the conviction that something in the undergraduate experience will lead to a more competent, more concerned, more complete human being.[19]

In the West, the idea of the liberal arts education was reborn with Renaissance scholars who, between 1300 and 1500, discovered lost scrolls and texts of ancient Greek and Latin writers. Based on these old teachings, they designed a new curriculum for students, first in Renaissance Italy, then throughout Western Europe and the New World. By the fifteenth century, the Italians called it *studia humanitatis*. It included grammar, rhetoric, poetry, and history. A sixteenth century teacher or student of the humanities was called a *humanista.*[20]

German historians coined the term "humanism" in the eighteenth century to define the emphasis on Greek and Latin classics in secondary education and to distinguish this from the rising demands for a more practical and scientific training.[21]

To graduate well-rounded, complete citizens, classical scholars required students to develop a working knowledge of what preceded them, indeed, what caused them to be.

Boyer, offering his recipe for a good general education today, also suggested studying the past, among other subjects:

> In an age when planned obsolescence seems to make everything but the fleeting moment remote and irrelevant, the study of history can strengthen awareness of tradition, of heritage, of meaning beyond the present, without which there is no culture. It is imperative that all students learn about women and men and the events and ideas that have contributed consequentially to our own history and to other cultures.[22]

There is a less philosophical, more practical reason to include history in a general education. People who know their own history are less likely to be fooled by periodic tyrants who assume power and try to rewrite it. Here are two examples of an attempt to rewrite history.

In the early years of the Soviet Union, Mikhail Pokovsky was a prominent historian. But Pokovsky offended Russian nationalists by including in his works contributions made by Vikings and Mongols. When Joseph Stalin (1879-1953) came to power in 1924, he insisted upon a history that glorified the Soviet Union as the world's leader in Communism and social and economic progress. "History" could give credit only to Slavic people. It had to speak in friendly terms about patriotism and love of the homeland. Stalin arbitrarily decided questions long debated by scholars. History became official propaganda; alternative accounts were prohibited.

In the United States, the victory of the Communists in China in 1949 caused a bitter controversy to erupt over who would interpret the events within China to Americans. Throughout World War II, Foreign Service officers in China reported that Chiang Kai-Shek's Nationalist government, which the United States supported, was corrupt and unpopular. They warned that Chiang's government would not survive a challenge from the Chinese Communists. When this occurred, proving these experts correct, powerful and influential men both in the United States government and out, who repeatedly had rejected the reports of the Foreign Service men, now looked for scapegoats. Who was to blame for "losing China?"

Joseph McCarthy (1908-1957), a junior senator from Wisconsin who was facing a re-election campaign, saw an opportunity to boost his political career. He falsely claimed he had lists containing names of Communists and their sympathizers within the State Department. He turned his attack on the very Foreign Service officers in China who had predicted the fall of the Nationalist government. McCarthy accused them of being Communist sympathizers and traitors to the United States government.

McCarthy became so powerful and reckless that he was instrumental in destroying the China Bureau of the State Department. He purged it of men who knew and understood Asia and had given years of honorable and faithful service to the State Department and the nation. For telling the truth about the situation in China, they were personally pilloried, and most of them were hounded out of government service altogether.

Those who replaced the men of the China Bureau learned a painful lesson: not to be the bearers of unpopular news or opinions. When the war in Vietnam began, there was a shortage of independent-minded Asian experts to interpret the situation for the State Department and the government. Those who could have done so had been purged by the junior senator from Wisconsin and the powerful men who used him for their own ends.

History may be used for all kinds of political and partisan advantage. It matters a great deal how the past is interpreted. Past events have shown repeatedly that it is dangerous to tamper with the facts.

From the Renaissance ideal, the West developed the concept of a broad liberal arts education. One of the goals of a Renaissance education was to produce educated, upright, rational, well-rounded, and employable individuals with a civic conscience that makes them good citizens of their world. That is still the goal of a liberal arts education. At its best, education opens windows of understanding and helps individuals become more tolerant, discerning, and respectful of different people. One of the paths to such understanding is the study of the past and how people came to be as they are.

HISTORY–SCIENCE OR NOT?

By the end of the seventeenth century, the scientific revolution had given many people a new way to look at the world. Laws of the universe were knowable, predictable, and unchanging. As historian E.H. Carr explained, it seemed that by using the proper methods of investigation, there was nothing humans could not learn and understand about themselves and their world. Scholars applied their new methods to many disciplines, including history. People wondered whether the same scientific methods, which worked so well in understanding nature, could be used to gain further knowledge about society itself.[23]

The scientific revolution took another step in 1859 when Charles Darwin published his theories about the origin and perpetuation of new species of animals and plants. Darwin demonstrated that science, like history, was involved with the process of change and development. His work also confirmed for many people the idea of progress in human history. In both science and history, people collected facts and interpreted them. By the beginning of the twentieth century, many were convinced that history was definitely a science.[24]

But history makes messy science. Two atoms of hydrogen and one of oxygen, properly bonded, always make water. But hungry peasants facing a harsh winter and high taxes might revolt, or they might not. They may wait until summer, when the weather is warmer. They might revolt against a monarch or they might ally with a monarch to condemn an upper class. Historians have been unsuccessful in their attempts to fit human society into a general set of laws.

Both scientists and historians have had to give up the idea that one day, if they searched hard enough, they would find an established, comprehensive body of knowledge that would settle all the questions once and for all.[25] By the end of the twentieth century, the goals are more realistic: "to advance from one hypothesis to another, isolating facts...."[26]

History is an important part of both the humanities and the social science disciplines of a university's liberal arts program. The researcher of humanities-oriented history may investigate journals, letters, and diaries for information on people and events. The social-science historian examines material such as census data, tax and voting records, or demographic records, which offers insight into a larger society.[27] Whatever the subject, it is important to use critical thinking, observation, and proof in writing history. Historians must find their answers by examining the facts. They must not jump to conclusions from prejudice or assumption. History and science both have the same goals: to expand human knowledge

CAREERS FOR HISTORY MAJORS

Many careers require people to process large amounts of information into usable parts. As a university graduate with a degree in history, you will have learned a number of invaluable skills that are marketable and attractive to future employers. You also have had the foundation of a liberal arts education which is not only a bonus in the job market but in itself will also enrich your life.

The American Historical Association published a book in 1977 called *Careers for Students of History*, that contains a list of these skills. They are:

1. analyze, interpret, and organize useful data
2. write with grammatical accuracy and clarity
3. prepare well documented reports
4. present an argument and debate it logically and succinctly
5. exercise originality and creativity in using research materials.[28]

The Information Age has greatly expanded the ways in which we communicate data. However, the written report still remains the standard in business, education, and government.[29] It is impossible to overemphasize how important are good communication skills, critical thinking, and the ability to use the English language correctly and well. These skills are of value to the business world in such areas as advertising, insurance, communications, publishing, banking, travel fields, and market research.[30] An attorney in law must have good research and writing skills and the ability to find past precedents that govern present cases.

The teaching profession has long been a traditionally rich market for graduates with a history degree. But a history graduate typically is required to have a teaching certificate to teach in most public schools. Your academic advisor can help you select the necessary courses to prepare you in this field. Requirements for teaching vary from state to state. You will need to inquire of the state in which you plan to work what, specifically, are the requirements for teaching.

The federal government also requires the skills of historians to compile and write histories for government agencies or the military. A historian might conduct research for study in foreign policy-making, analyze the use of natural resources for the Department of the Interior, or work in the development of the space program. Historical studies are used as a guide to future planning in many departments of government.[31]

In 1989, Dr. Barbara J. Howe, director of the Public History Program at West Virginia University, authored an updated and expanded volume of *Careers for Students of History*.[32] Besides chapters on careers in research and education, Dr. Howe explores the opportunities for history majors as writers and editors, information managers, advocates, businesspeople, and professionals. As information seekers, the historian's abilities and skills are essential to the Information Age.

CONCLUSION

The study of history helps to develop the skills to discover new knowledge. The ability to learn is necessary for the opportunity to change. Learning is a life-long process that enables people to live fuller lives and to master the challenges of the future. Well-educated liberal arts graduates in history should be limited only by their imaginations.

ENDNOTES

[1] Barbara Tuchman, *Practicing History* (New York: Alfred A. Knopf, 1981), 27, 28.

[2] Barbara Tuchman, *A Distant Mirror: The Calamitous 14th Century* (New York: Alfred A. Knopf, 1978), 292.

[3] Samuel Eliot Morison, *Oxford History of the American People* (New York: Oxford University Press, 1965), 23.

[4] Paul Leicester Ford, ed., *Writings of Christopher Columbus: Descriptive of the Discovery and Occupation of the New World* (New York: C.L. Webster & Company, 1892), 34, 42.

[5] Garry Wills, "Man of the Year," *New York Review of Books*, 21 November, 1991, 18.

[6] Kirkpatrick Sale, *The Conquest of Paradise: Christopher Columbus and the Columbian Legacy* (New York: Penguin Books, 1991), 161.

[7] William W. Borah, *Justice by Insurance: The General Indian Count of Colonial Mexico and the Legal Aides of the Half-Real* (Berkeley: University of California Press, 1983), 26; quoted in Mark Burkholder and Lyman Johnson, *Colonial Latin America* (Oxford University Press, 1990), 99.

[8] Will and Ariel Durant, *The Lessons of History* (New York: Simon and Shuster, 1968), 52.

[9] Reuven Frank, quoted in Jeffrey Frank, "When Truth Becomes Image Becomes History Becomes Myth," *The Washington Post Weekly*, 11-17 May 1992, 24.

[10]*Ibid.*

[11]Walter Cronkite, quoted in Don Oberdorfer, *Tet!* (Garden City, New York: Doubleday & Company, Inc., 1971), 158.

[12]Sean Wilentz, "Tales of Hoffa," *The New Republic*, 1 February 1993, 53.

[13]George Kitson Clark, *The Critical Historian* (New York: Basic Books, 1967), 45.

[14]Thucydides, *History of the Peloponnesian War*, translated by Rex Warner (London: Penguin Books, 1954), 24.

[15]Stephen Jay Gould, *Hen's Teeth and Horse's Toes* (New York: W.W. Norton & Company, 1983), 122, 123.

[16]Paul Gagnon, "Why Study History?," *The Atlantic Monthly*, November 1988, 44.

[17]Richard Neustadt and Ernest May, *Thinking in Time: The Uses of History for Decision Makers* (New York: Macmillan Company, 1986), 92.

[18]Edward Hallett Carr, *What is History?* (New York, Random House, 1961), 142.

[19]Ernest L. Boyer, The Carnegie Foundation for the Advancement of Teaching, *College: The Undergraduate Experience in America* (New York: Harper & Row, 1987), 1.

[20]Paul Kristeller, *Renaissance Thought* (New York: Harper & Row, 1955), 9.

[21]W. Rüegg, *Cicero und der Humanismus* (Zurich, 1946), Iff.; quoted in Paul Kristeller, *Renaissance Thought* (New York: Harper & Row, 1955), 9.

[22]Boyer, *College: The Undergraduate Experience*, 94.

[23]Carr, *What is History?*, 70.

[24]*Ibid.*, 71.

[25]*Ibid.*, 77.

[26]*Ibid.*

[27]Barbara J. Howe, *Careers for Students of History* (Washington: American Historical Association, 1989), 2, 3.

[28]Sally Gregory Kohlstedt, ed., *Careers for Students of History* (Washington: American Historical Association, 1977), ix.

[30]*Ibid.*, 40, 43.

[31]*Ibid.*, 21.

[32]Howe, *Careers for Students of History*, 1-94.

BIBLIOGRAPHY

Boyer, Ernest L. The Carnegie Foundation for the Advancement of Teaching. *College: The Undergraduate Experience in America*. New York: Harper & Row, Publishers, 1987.

Breisach, Ernest. *Historiography*. Chicago: The University of Chicago Press, 1983.

Burke, Peter. *New Perspectives on Historical Writing*. University Park, Pennsylvania: The Pennsylvania State University Press, 1991.

Burkholder, Mark and Lyman Johnson. *Colonial Latin America*. Oxford: Oxford University Press, 1990.

Carr, Edward Hallett. *What is History?* New York: Random House, 1961.

Durant, Will and Ariel. *The Lessons of History*. New York: Simon and Schuster, 1968.

Darnton, Robert. "An Enlightened Revolution?" *New York Review of Books*, 24 October 1991, 33-36.

Davidson, James and Mark Lytle. *After the Fact*. New York: Alfred A. Knopf, 1982.

Ford, Paul Leicester, ed. *Writings of Christopher Columbus: Descriptive of the Discovery and Occupation of the New World*. New York: C.L. Webster & Company, 1892.

Frank, Jeffrey. "When Truth Becomes Image Becomes History Becomes Myth." *The Washington Post Weekly*, 11-17 May 1992.

Gagnon, Paul. "Why Study History?" *The Atlantic Monthly*, November 1988.

Gardiner, Juliet, ed. *What is History Today?* Atlantic Highlands, New Jersey: Humanities Press International, Inc., 1988.

Gould, Stephen Jay. *Hen's Teeth and Horse's Toes*. New York: W.W. Norton & Company, 1983.

Howe, Barbara J. *Careers for Students of History*. Washington: American Historical Association, 1989.

Kammen, Michael, ed. "What is the Good of History?" Selected

Letters of Carl L. Becker, 1900-1945. Ithaca: Cornell University Press, 1973.

Kitson Clark, George. *The Critical Historian.* New York: Basic Books, Inc., Publishers, 1967.

Kohlstedt, Sally Gregory, ed. *Careers for Students of History.* Washington: American Historical Association, 1977.

Kristeller, Paul. *Renaissance Thought.* New York: Harper & Row, Publishers, 1955.

Morison, Samuel Eliot. *Oxford History of the American People.* New York: Oxford University Press, 1965.

Neustadt, Richard and Ernest May. *Thinking in Time: The Uses of History for Decision Makers.* New York: Macmillan, 1986.

Oberdorfer, Don. *Tet!* Garden City, New York: Doubleday & Company, Inc., 1971.

Sale, Kirkpatrick. *The Conquest of Paradise: Christopher Columbus and the Columbian Legacy.* New York: Penguin Books, 1991.

Thucydides, *History of the Peloponnesian War.* Translated by Rex Warner. London: Penguin Books, 1954.

Tuchman, Barbara W. *A Distant Mirror: The Calamitous Fourteenth Century.* New York: Alfred A. Knopf, 1978.

———. *Practicing History.* New York: Alfred A. Knopf, 1981.

Wilentz, Sean. "Tales of Hoffa." *The New Republic*, 1 February 1993, 53-60.

Wills, Garry. "Man of the Year." *The New York Review of Books*, 21 November 1991.

CHAPTER TWO

USING THE LIBRARY

INTRODUCTION

Entering a college or university library for the first time may be an intimidating experience. This may be the largest library you have ever visited. Happily, there is access to almost everything you need to accomplish your academic tasks.

University libraries employ highly trained professional librarians to assist you in your work. Never hesitate to seek assistance from a librarian, for they are the most helpful sources of information in the library. A conversation with a reference librarian will give you a good start as you begin your acquaintance with a university library.

REFERENCE ROOM

Research for any history project begins in the library **reference room**. Housed in this area are thousands of research aids, indices, directories, data bases, and the all-important card catalog. These materials serve two purposes. First, they help you to define and narrow your research topics. Second, they direct you to the appropriate sources of material for your history projects. You will use these resource tools throughout your years of study.

The reference room of a large university library may seem overwhelming at first glance. Take a few minutes to look around. A large and obvious feature is the familiar **card catalog**, housed in numerous small wooden drawers on alphabetized paper cards which identify and locate book holdings of the library.

Some libraries, however, now have a computerized card catalog operated from terminals at all branches of the university's libraries. These on-line systems rely on a computer which provides access to all the book collections in every library on campus. Most systems even indicate whether or not a book has been checked out.

Computerized card catalogs offer the operator a variety of ways to search for relevant materials: by subject, title, author, keyword in the title, Dewey Call Number, or Library of Congress Call Number. Each terminal displays operating instructions on how to gain access to the book listings contained in the database. If you are reluctant to use a computerized card catalog system, or if your search has not turned up materials useful for your research, ask for help. The reference librarian can get you started or help you to refine your search.

In addition to the card catalog, the reference room contains many volumes in series. These are **indices** (also called indexes). An index is a systematic guide to academic publications. The *Reader's Guide to Periodical Literature* is a well-known index of popular magazines and scholarly journals. You probably used it or other indices while you were in high school. Some of the indices are in paper or soft cover. So much material is published each month that indices must be updated monthly, quarterly, or annually. These guides index academic studies in a variety of ways. All indices offer subject directories. Many will index by title and some by author. Items may be located by several methods. The most productive way to search an index is by subject.

Indices are frequently cross-referenced under many different subject headings. For example, a book about midwives in Kansas during the Progressive Era of American History may be found under the subject headings "midwives," "Kansas," and "Progressive Era." Keep this in mind as you search these indices for works related to your history project.

Not all of the books you see in the reference room are indices of the type described above. Some are specific to particular publications. Two important newspapers, *The New York Times* and *The Times* of London, which we commonly call *The London Times* both furnish an index of their daily publications. If you need to know the English Prime Minister's response to a speech that the President of the United States made, you can go to the *Official Index to the Times [of London]* and look up articles on that subject.

In addition to the electronic card catalog in the reference room, a number of other computers are available to students. These computers are equipped to search **databases**. Databases are huge collections of information contained on small computer discs. One disc can hold 250,000 pages of information. Like indices, these databases can be used to search publications. Well-known examples of databases are *ERIC*, which indexes sociology and education journals, and *Academic Index*, a guide to general and social science publications. The trend today is toward transferring indices to database because they take up less room in already overcrowded libraries. If the index you are examining appears to stop suddenly, ask a reference librarian if it is continued on a database.

There are thousands of specialized aids in the reference room. Many of these books will be of great value to you. As you research your topic, you may have questions about well-known people. To find out more about them, look at the *Dictionary of American Biography* or *Biographical Sources for Foreign Countries*. If you are interested in the public response to a book you are reading, the *Book Review Digest* or the *Index to Book Reviews in the Humanities* will be useful. If you need support for an argument you are making about conditions in an area during a particular period of history, the *Historical Statistics of the United States*, or, for Latin America, the *Statistical Abstract of Latin America* provides data. These are a few examples of the valuable reference books available in the library. There is almost certainly a book there to help you find the information you need, you just have to locate it.

To be a successful student you need a general knowledge of

how the library system works and a specific understanding of the most important tools in your discipline. Beyond that level of competency, *ask for help from the reference librarian.* Do not overlook an important source because you were too shy to ask for assistance.

To put to use some of this new information, we will use two examples as models to examine the research process, beginning at the familiar paper card catalog available in every library.

EXAMPLES

In your history classes often you are permitted some freedom in the choice of topics for research projects. Pretend that you have been brave enough to enroll in two history classes this semester and are assigned to write two research papers. Because you are diligent, dedicated, and a bit frightened, you hurry to the library on the first day of class to get started on your research. One of the courses in which you are enrolled is a history of the United States from the nineteenth century to the present and the other is a survey of Western Civilization from the Renaissance to the present.

In order to get an early start on your research you choose topics for both papers. The women's rights movement interests you, so you plan to do your United States paper on that. Not knowing much about the Nazi military machine during World War II, you select that subject as your topic for the Western Civilization course. Armed with your decisions, you approach the card catalog and begin your search for books.

THE CARD CATALOG

The card catalog is an excellent place to begin your research. As you flip through the cards under "women's rights," you discover a multitude of cards relating to the women's rights movement that do not satisfy the image that you have of the issue. There are too many books related to the topic and too many cards dealing with subjects you do not understand. In addition to the cards classified under "women's rights," there are many subdivisions subdivisions: "Asia," "Australia," "Bibliographies," "Congresses," "England," "Europe," "France," and the "United States." Upon examining the cards on "women's rights ‑ United States," you are distressed to find that it, too, has subcategories! What to do? What is the difference between the women's rights movement and the suffrage movement? Was the Equal Rights Amendment of the 1920s the same one discussed today? What does the Equal Rights Amendment guarantee? What is the women's rights movement?

Frustrated, you decide to pursue your Western Civilization topic instead. First you look under "Nazi" and find a few cards for books on the subject, but none of them deal with Nazi military strategy. Are these books all that the library has on the Nazi movement? It does not appear to be much of a collection. There is a card at the beginning of the section which says, "See National Socialism." An examination of the cards in that section reveals numerous books by and about Adolf Hitler. There are also several books about the political philosophy of National Socialism, but nothing on the Nazi army. Again, now what?

These examples reveal the two most common problems that students face when approaching a card catalog to look for information. With the women's rights topic you were lucky to discover that there were a large number of books available on the general topic, but because you have no clear and precise focus for your paper, you do not know which of these books is appropriate for you. Before going any further in your research for this paper you need to make some decisions about what your topic is going to be. Are you interested in the women's rights movement of the nineteenth century, the suffrage movement of the early twentieth century, the feminist campaigns of the 1960s and 1970s, or women's rights in the 1990s? Say that you decide on the nineteenth century. Now that you have limited your topic, you can go back to the card catalog and find one or two books to give you a start.

The problem with the Nazi topic is different. Instead of having too many possible entries, there seems to be little on the Nazi military machine. Where do you go from here? The *Library of Congress Subject Headings* are four books containing a published list of subject headings found in the card catalog. If you can not find a topic in the card catalog, go to these books to uncover alternative subject headings. Here is how the *Library of Congress Subject Headings* books work in locating material for the Nazi topic.

If you begin with the word, "Nazi," you will find that there is nothing about the military under Hitler. There are, however, a number of unexplained abbreviations under the major heading. These abbreviations and their meanings are as follows:

> UF means "used for." This symbol denotes terms with the same meaning *which are not used*. They are *not* subject headings, but they are placed with subject headings which reveal the same information.
>
> BT is the abbreviation for "broad term." This is a more general but closely connected subject heading which will provide related information.
>
> RT stands for "related term." Consider these headings because they suggest other possible categories to explore.
>
> SA means "see above." These are headings which will lead you to other related information.
>
> NT is a symbol for "narrow topic." Unlike the

broader categories above, these narrow topics will help you focus on specific headings related to larger issues you are pursuing.

Keeping this information in mind, an examination of possible terms related to "Nazi" illustrates how this works. You have looked under "Nazi" and "National Socialism" and found nothing. You must widen your card catalog search. Turn to the heading, "Germany." Under that category are several pages of citations. The beginning of the entry looks like this:

Germany (Not Subd Geog)
  Here are entered works on Germany for the pre-1949 period, the Territories under Allied Occupation, and East Germany and West Germany, collectively, for the post-1949 period, as well as works on Germany since reunification in 1990.

    NT Germany (East)
     Germany (West)
      -Antiquities (Not Subd Geog)
        NT Bedburg-Konigshoven Site (Germany)
          Fesstalle Rockshelter (Germany)
          Grosse Grotte (Germany)
          Haithabu (Extinct City)
          Hardburg bei Istein Site (Germany)
          Kleebergschacht Cave (Germany)
          Klein-Aspergle Mound (Germany)
          Rohnstedt Site (Germany)
          Wusterhusen Site (Germany)
     -Antiquities, Roman
     -Armed Forces (May Subd Geog)
       --Medals, badges, decorations, etc.
         NT Deutsche Kreuz (Medal)

      Orden Pour Le Merite
  -Boundaries
    --Poland
      NT Oder-Neisse Line (Germany and Poland)
  -Capital and Capitol
  -Church History
    --to 843
    --Middle Ages, 843-1517
     NT Stedingers
    --16th century
    --17th century
    --18th century

The entries listed under "Germany" continue for two more pages.

In examining this entry from the *Library of Congress Subject Headings*, notice that the abbreviations mentioned above are used throughout this citation. The letters "NT" are particularly useful. By pointing to narrower topics under the heading of "Germany," the book serves as a guide to help you to narrow your own research topic. At the beginning of most lengthy entries is a brief explanation of the subjects listed under that heading. Be sure to read this paragraph. Notice also whether topics are subdivided by geographical regions, indicated by "Subd Geog."

A careful examination of the subject, "Germany" suggests that your most fruitful effort will be found under the heading, "World War II." There you discover two "NT" (narrow topic) citations: "World War II, 1939-1945 -- Campaigns," and "World War II, 1939-1945 -- Operations." These sound promising. Back at the card catalog, you discover a number of books with titles appropriate to the German Army during World War II. Also, German History has chronological divisions with entries on the Nazi movement and World War II. After locating and examining some of the available books, you narrow your research topic to the German invasion of the Soviet Union in 1941.

To produce an effective research paper, there is no substitute or shortcut for these steps. Carefully choose a subject about which you are interested. Skim several relevant books and think about your topic. Narrow and define it as much as you can. This will help you organize your research more efficiently, save time, and make the whole process more manageable and satisfactory. Throughout the research process, you may decide to narrow and limit your subject still further as you assemble your information.

USING THE CARD CATALOG

Now that you have narrowed your topics and have found related subject headings in the card catalog, take a few minutes to learn how the card catalog works. Here is a sample author card from the catalog.

HQ1236.5
.U6B69   Boydston, Jeanne
1988   The Limits of Sisterhood: The Beecher Sisters on Women's
            Sphere/ Jeanne Boydston, Mary Kelley, Anne Margolis.--
            Chapel Hill: University of North Carolina Press, c1988.
                xxiv, 369 p.: ill., port.; 24cm.
                -- (Gender and American Culture)
                Includes bibliographical references and index.
                ISBN 0-8078 - 1788 - 6
    1. Women's rights-- United States-- History-- 19th century--
Sources. 2. Feminism-- United States-- History - 19th century--
Sources. 3. Beecher, Catherine Ester, 1800-1878. 4. Stowe, Harriet
Beecher, 1811-1896. 5. Hooker, Isabella Beecher, 1822-1907. I.
Kelley, Mary, 1943- II. Margolis, Anne Throne. III. Title.

TYPES OF CARDS IN THE CARD CATALOG

In the early stages of your research, you will find most of your books in the card catalog by following the subject headings. However each book is listed on three different types of cards in the card catalog: subject, author, and title. Once you find a book that looks particularly promising, take a moment to examine the author card of that book. This card carries suggestions for other subject headings which may be of use to you.

There is much other helpful information on the author card. The top line of the card names the author who is given credit for the work. On the other two cards for this book, this line would reveal either the subject of the book or its title. The example indicates that Jeanne Boydston wrote the book. The title is on the next line of the card. Names of books on these cards are not underlined, so be careful to write down the full and correct title of the book.

The information that follows the title is significant because it contains all that you need to know to create either a bibliographic entry or a footnote. In addition to the primary author, Jeanne Boydston, Mary Kelley and Anne Margolis contributed to this work. *The Limits of Sisterhood* was published by the University of North Carolina at Chapel Hill in 1988. This data provides all the necessary information to satisfy whichever method of citation you are following. We will discuss bibliographies and footnotes in the next chapter.

The information below the publication section is a physical description of the book. In this case, the introduction is twenty-four pages long (xxiv) and the body of the work contains 369 pages. The illustrations in the book are portraits. The book is twenty-four centimeters tall. It contains bibliographical references and an index. The *International Standard Book Number* (ISBN), the ten digit number at the bottom of the card, is useful only to librarians and book dealers when ordering books. It is not important to us.

The numbered sections on the bottom of the card are called

tracings. Tracings are the other headings under which this book is found in the card catalog. In our catalog card sample, subject cards for *The Limits of Sisterhood* are found under "Women's Rights," "Feminism," "Catherine Beecher," "Harriet Beecher Stowe," and "Isabella Beecher Hooker." Subheadings and dates are also provided. Additional author cards are found under the names Mary Kelley and Anne Throne Margolis. Finally, a title card is also in the catalog.

CALL NUMBERS

The letter and number combination on the left of the card, the **call numbers**, directs you to the location of the book. While most libraries have maps to direct you where to find books, it is helpful to acquaint yourself with the classification system in use.

Most college libraries use the **Library of Congress Classification System**, a system of 21 letters which define broad topics. These are refined by the addition of a second letter and then by a number to further distinguish books which share letters. For example: history books are found under the letters D, E, and F. Books on the history of France carry the second letter C. Therefore a book on French history will have a call number beginning with the letters DC.

Examine the sample card above. Notice that the call number for the book on women's history does not begin with D, E, or F. Many books that are related to historical subjects are classified under Social Sciences. This broad topic, which includes books on social history and women's history, is assigned the letter, H.

As you write down the call number, be careful to note any special abbreviations above it. If present, these may represent a special collection or a different library where this book is housed. The most frequent abbreviation is the letter R, or "Ref;" this denotes a book that is in the reference room. When in doubt about any notation, ask the reference room librarian for assistance.

After accurately recording the call number, and with a library map in hand, you are ready to go into the stacks to locate the book you have chosen. **Stacks** is a technical name given to the seemingly endless shelves of books which house the library's collections. Once you arrive on the proper floor, detailed floor plan maps located near elevators and staircases will point you to the correct call number location. Find the first letter of the call number, then the second letter. Next, search for the digits which immediately follow the first letters. The letters following that first combination of letters and numbers will be arranged in alphabetical order. All of the As will be placed together before the ABs begin, just as all of the 1s will be combined in a section before the 1.1s start. Doing this is much easier than reading about it, so go to the stacks and look around for a few minutes. You will quickly discover that this method of finding books is quite simple.

INITIAL RESEARCH

Before you begin your research, read all references to your chosen topics in your class textbooks. These books contain general information that places each subject within the context of its period of history. If you need more of this background information, the *Encyclopedia of the Social Sciences* may be helpful.

Now that you have found and checked out a few books, your research is underway. The narrowing process begins as you skim these first reference books. Focus your attention on one time period, event, issue, or individual connected with your topic that really interests you. Look through the indices of your library books and begin collecting information. You should also spend some time doing **footnote research**.

Reading through the footnotes at the bottom of pages or endnotes at the back of the book will provide you with valuable information for your research. The author of your library book has written about your topic and has spent months or years engaged in the same sort of research that you are now doing. By looking at his or her footnotes you will find a number of sources which will be useful to you. Once you begin to find appropriate references, and locate and read them yourself in the library, you will discover that every new source will lead you to another potential source of information.

A word of warning, however: be selective in the sources that you examine. Many books may appear interesting, but you must limit yourself to those sources of information that particularly focus on your chosen topic. Carefully consider the material in the footnotes you read. Make sure that it supports parts of the text that are related to the topic you have chosen. Try to avoid spending time chasing down irrelevant books and articles. If, after a reasonable time, you are still undecided about how to narrow your topic, ask your professor for suggestions.

JOURNAL RESEARCH

Scholarly journals are academic publications that not only contain the latest available information but also offer a wealth of material about historical events and academic trends that influence the study of history. Scholarly journals also contain reviews of new books and documentary collections. Competent research includes investigation of one or more journals that are relevant to your chosen topic.

Be careful not to confuse a scholarly journal with a popular magazine. They are not interchangeable sources of information. For example, *Newsweek*, *Time*, or *U.S. News and World Report* occasionally may contain interesting historical articles, but they are not scholarly journals. They are popular news magazines, available at newsstands everywhere, that are designed to inform the general public on a wide variety of subjects.

A scholarly journal is purchased by subscription and has a smaller readership. The *Journal of American History*, *Past and Present*, *History Today*, *Slavic Review*, *Political Science Quarterly*, *Labor History*, *Hispanic American Historical Review*, *Journal of Modern History*, and *Foreign Affairs*, are a very few of the many scholarly journals available for historical research in libraries. They may be unfamiliar to you. As you begin your research, now is a good time to become acquainted with both the journals and the methods by which you locate useful information in them.

HISTORICAL INDICES

Using academic journals is a three step process which begins with an examination of **historical indices**. A list of useful indices is included in an appendix at the back of this book. To begin a search through any index, *go to the front of the volume and read the instructions for its use.*

There is a very large amount of information available on most historical issues. Because you have already considered a more narrowly defined topic (event, person, or time period) for your research paper on the German Army in World War II – the Nazi assault on the Soviet Union in 1941 – you are able to focus your search for journal articles on that particular subject.

Historical Abstracts, and its companion book, *America: History and Life*, are arranged essentially the same way. For German army articles, begin with the book, *Historical Abstracts*. This publication and its index are arranged in two sections. The first is *Modern History Abstracts, 1450-1914*. The second is *Twentieth Century Abstracts*. The index is also divided into these two time periods. The *Twentieth Century Abstracts* will contain information for sources on Germany during World War II.

A cumulative index to *Historical Abstracts* is published every five years to make research easier. Select the most recent five year index and turn to the entries listed under the subject heading, "Germany." You will find many pages of entries, alphabetized by key word. For your research, "Military strategy" contains useful information that will lead you to several abstracts of journal articles. To locate them, you must note the alphanumerical combination listed at each entry.

The first number is the volume number. The letter that follows it indicates in which of the two collections of abstracts it will be found. The letter "A" indicates an entry in *Modern History Abstracts*. Entries in *Twentieth Century Abstracts* are always marked with a "B." Following the colon is a number which represents the particular abstract you should examine. For example, the entry, 34B:369 refers to abstract 369 in volume 34 of *Twentieth Century Abstracts*. That selection is a short synopsis of the article, "Hitler's Late Summer Pause in 1941."

Finding the abstract of an article in a scholarly journal is the first step in this process. Next, read the abstract and determine if the article will help you with your research paper. If so, you must locate the journal which contains the entire article. Carefully note the titles of both the article and the journal, as well as the volume and page numbers. All this information is located in the abstract you have just read. Now you are prepared to check the *Union List of Serials*.

The *Union List* is a listing of all the journals and periodicals that the library owns. This list will tell you if the journal you need is available in the library and where it is located. As with books, if there are no special abbreviations above the call number, then the call numbers of journals in the *Union List* indicate the journals' location. Like series of journals or magazines are bound together to form books called **bound serials**. They are housed in the stacks. **Unbound serials** are the most recent journals. They have not yet been bound together, and most of them are in a **current periodicals room** where they can be read in individual copies. When you locate the article, take notes on pertinent information that you find there. Some libraries permit you to check out journals overnight or to photocopy particularly important articles for your research.

The first time you follow this procedure to locate a scholarly journal article, it will seem an awkward, time-consuming, and difficult process. With practice, it becomes easier. If you have difficulty at any point, a reference librarian stands ready to assist you.

NEWSPAPER RESEARCH

To this point, we have dealt with **secondary sources**. Secondary sources are books and other publications that offer information and a written analysis about an event after it has occurred. **Primary sources**, on the other hand, are contemporary accounts or records of an event or issue. The Constitution of the United States is a primary source. However, historian Charles Beard's famous writings which analyze the Constitution are secondary sources. The transcripts of Clarence Thomas' confirmation hearings are a primary source. *People* magazine's article on Justice Thomas is a secondary source from a popular magazine.

Newspapers, while they may be biased, provide contemporary accounts of events as they happen. Therefore, newspapers are excellent primary sources because they reveal how people actually understood events that were taking place during their lives. Because they provide such useful information, they should be included in your research material whenever possible.

There are many newspapers published everyday. If you are interested in local events or local reactions to national and international occurrences, ask a librarian for help in locating indices for regional newspapers. To explore two of the most influential newspapers in the world, inspect the *Official Index to the Times* that indexes the *London Times*, and the *New York Times Index*. These indices are simpler to use than are *Historical Abstracts*. Each volume of these indices catalogs one year of their respective newspapers. To find an article, search the index for the citation and copy the date of the article and the page number. The *New York Times Index* also describes the length of the article and indicates in which section of the newspaper it is located.

With the date in hand, find the library's newspaper collection. Newspapers take up a great deal of space and deteriorate quickly in storage. Therefore, all but the most recent issues are on **microform**. Microform is a generic term applied to the product that is produced by photographing hard copy material and reproducing it in much smaller form on opaque film. The film may come on rolls – **microfilm** – or on sheets called **microfiche**. However the newspapers have been copied, you must use a special machine, either a **microfiche or microfilm reader**, to read the material. Microfilm collections and the equipment to use them have a special location in the library. The reference room librarian will direct you to the collection.

OTHER PRIMARY SOURCES

A good research paper contains a combination of primary and secondary sources. Finding and using primary sources is no more difficult than locating secondary sources for your paper. Careful reading of catalog cards, bibliographies, and footnotes will lead you to primary sources. *The Limits of Sisterhood*, the card example from the card catalog, contains original source materials. If you will refer back to it you will see that the first tracing (the numbered items at the bottom of the card), includes the word "sources," indicating that primary materials are included in this book. By noting the tracings on author cards on every book you choose for research, your primary source material will be easily available.

Many kinds of primary sources are useful to historical research. Autobiographies, personal diaries, speeches, photographs, eyewitness accounts by a person's friend, colleague, or opponent, are all documents that contain first hand information and are primary source materials. Research topics as widely diverse as our examples — the nineteenth century women's movement in the United States and the German army's attack on the Soviet Union in 1941 — each offer an opportunity to use a variety of primary sources.

GOVERNMENT DOCUMENTS

Much useful information about both American and World history is contained in material published by government agencies. Both the United States and foreign governments produce a large amount of printed material about their countries, particularly in the area of foreign policy. Military records are also valuable tools. For example, for your research paper on the German army, you should examine the daily *Diary of the German High Command*.

A particularly useful collection of primary sources are those documents printed by the United States government. These documents are published at public expense by government agencies. They include records of government administration, statistics gathered by public officials, and research projects funded by public money. The United States government publishes an incredible amount of information in their own printing facility, the Government Printing Office. To make this information available to the public, a special **regional depository system** has been established. Libraries that are designated regional depositories receive a copy of each publication issued by the Government Printing Office. Most large state universities act in this capacity.

The availability of all these informative publications is a real asset for historical research. Using government documents is somewhat different than using the card catalog or a serials index. While some public documents have been incorporated into the card catalog system, most have not. To utilize these materials you must begin by examining the *Catalog of the United States Government Publications* or the *Cumulative Subject Index to the Monthly Catalog of the United States Government Publications*. The *Monthly Catalog* indexes each month's publications and is compiled each year into an annual index. The *Cumulative Subject Index* covers government material printed between 1900 and 1971.

When you examine these indices, you will realize that they are related to both the card catalog and a serials index. After locating your topic in the Monthly Catalog, you will find an entry number which will lead you to a main entry. By going to that main entry, you will find **a Superintendent of Documents classification**. This number is the one that the librarian will use to retrieve your document. Few libraries permit open access to government documents. However, librarians will assist you in finding what you need. Government documents are invaluable primary sources that you should not overlook as you seek out research materials. For topics outside the borders of the United States, remember that the federal government finances studies of foreign nations, so these documents may still contain helpful source materials.

OTHER RESOURCE TOOLS

In this chapter we have just begun to explore the research tools available to you in your college library. To further assist you, a lengthy appendix of significant reference books is included at the back of this book. Also in the library reference room is the book, *Guide to Reference Books*. By looking under your topic, you should be able to locate reference materials to assist you with any inquiry. For example, under the heading, "Germany, 20th Century," there are several bibliographic sources listed which might prove useful with the paper on the German Army.

While the *Guide to Reference Books* and the other resources mentioned are valuable resource aids, remember that reference librarians are the most helpful feature of the library. Never hesitate to request their assistance with any research question or problem that you might encounter.

CONCLUSION

Now that you have begun to use the library's resources and to gather material for your papers, you are ready to start thinking about writing. The first step to good writing is good, careful, solid research. In the next chapter we will discuss reading and note taking, and the steps necessary to move from a pile of note cards to a finished paper.

CHAPTER THREE

WRITING FOR HISTORY CLASSES

PART ONE – WRITING A RESEARCH PAPER

Introduction

The purpose of writing is to communicate information in a clear, persuasive, and well-organized manner. Learning how to do so is an important part of a college education that will be valuable to you throughout your life. Good writing requires serious thought, hard work, and more time than you think it will. Some people have a talent for expressing themselves through writing, others do not. However, with perserverence, everyone can learn to write better. Writing is a creative process, with the end result a work that is uniquely your own.

In the last chapter, we discussed how to locate the appropriate research materials to write a history paper. Now we will focus on the process of reading those materials, assimilating the information, and putting the data together with your own original thought to produce a quality research paper. We also will consider briefly how to take notes, and write essays and identifications for history examinations.

Reading The Documents You Have Gathered

Careful preparation for writing your history research paper is essential – there are few short-cuts. You have collected an impressive stack of books, scholarly journal articles, newspaper clippings, and primary-source documents. But effective research requires more than just finding and compiling lists of related items: you must develop the ability to cull through these materials and discern what information is most relevant to your topics.

Read your materials carefully. This is the key to getting the most from your collected sources. The only way to write a good research paper is to read! However, reading must be more than a random activity. Be selective in what you read. Make sure that your chosen books or articles are directly related to your topic. Be prepared, upon closer examination, to reject any that are not. Make a habit of reading the author's introduction and the table of contents, and skimming the indices of the books you have chosen. These provide keys to the focus of the book, the arrangement of the subjects, and their numbers and locations. Ignore any material not relevant to your chosen research topic. Remember, you have a lifetime to read all sorts of interesting things; you have only one semester to research and write your paper.

In using library books, you will discover that students before you have carelessly vandalized many of them by marking them with pens and highlighters, and by turning down or even tearing out pages. Aside from the costs involved, many damaged books cannot be replaced because they are out of print. Regardless of how wide-spread this practice appears to be, it is wrong. Also, it is lazy research and ultimately self-defeating, for it is a disorganized, time-consuming, and inefficient way of gathering information.

Taking Research Notes

No one is capable of keeping track of large volumes of information without assistance. To aid you in remembering the most important facts, you must take **research notes** as you read. Good notes serve several purposes: they enable you to recall the original source from which you gathered the information; they include broad headings that will help you to organize your information as you write; and they include specific facts, opinions, or quotes that you consider important to your subject.

Scholars through the years have found that the **index card** is a reliable tool in the research process. Index cards come in several sizes. Select cards that will provide you enough room to include all the data you consider significant. Be consistent in the size of your cards for each project. Trying to keep 3"x5" and 4"x6" cards together at the same time is awkward.

Avoid the temptation to take notes on legal pads or in notebooks. Initially it may be easier to keep track of your notes this way, but it will be impossible to organize and difficult to retrieve your information when you attempt to write. Turning page after page in an effort to locate a particular reference is more inefficient and frustrating than having all your related cards collected in individual piles at your side.

The following sample note card, using material from a book for the research paper on the women's rights movement which was discussed in Chapter 2, demonstrates the types of information you will need to include on all of your cards.

Broad Heading – Women's Groups who supported suffrage across racial as well as gender lines.

Specific – Women's group "Sorosis" advocated "Universal Suffrage and equal Rights for all the People," Chicago 1869.

Source – Buechler, *The Transformation of the Woman Suffrage Movement*. (Page Number) p. 69.

On the card, notice that there are two separate notations. In this example, "Women's groups who supported suffrage (the right to vote) across racial as well as gender lines" is the **broad heading** of your index card. A strong research paper is based on a number of facts that support broad assertions. As you read, you will find other important categories, or time-periods, people, or occurrences, that make appropriate broad-headings for your topic.

A **specific fact** about the issue indicated on the broad heading card is described in the second notation. Use a separate index card for each specific fact, idea, or quotation. Keep together the information you collect that relates to each broad heading.

In addition to the relevant fact that you have gathered from this book, you have listed on your index card the information necessary to create a **footnote** and a **bibliographic entry** to show the **source** of your information: the author's or authors' names, title of the source, and page number on which you found the information.

Occasionally a phrase or sentence in your reading is so pertinent and well-written, or such a good example of some point you are making, that you want to use the author's exact words in your paper. This is called a **direct quote**. Be sure that you copy the author's exact words on your index card, and that you have not changed the author's meaning by taking the sentence out of context. In your research paper, do not use too many direct quotes nor use them as a substitute for doing your own thinking.

Let us say that you have narrowed the focus of your American history paper to this topic: the relationship between women's suffrage and the extension of voting rights to other disenfranchised members of society (those deprived of the right to vote) during the quarter-century following the Civil War. In searching for information on the topics, "women's suffrage" and "voting rights" between 1865 and 1890, you read of an organization in Chicago called "Sorosis," which advocated suffrage for women. You have found a **lead** to new information – the name of a group that appears to be important to the issues at hand. You have never heard of them before. What information might you gather about them that would increase your understanding of women's suffrage and voting rights in the post-Civil War period? Here are some possibilities:

What was the opinion of this group toward extending voting rights to minorities? Did their membership include people of color? Where did they stand on literacy as a test for the right to vote? Did they advocate universal suffrage? As you locate whatever information about Sorosis you decide is important to your research, write it on *individual index cards*. As you read on, other leads indicate that these kinds of questions also apply to groups and agencies who worked to extend voting rights to newly-freed African-Americans. Were the other groups also supportive of the women's suffrage movement? How did the Fourteenth Amendment (all persons born or naturalized in the United States are citizens with the right of equal protection under the law) influence them in their work? Did the Fifteenth Amendment (outlawing racial discrimination in voter rights) help the fight for women's suffrage?

If new material is pertinent to women's groups who supported suffrage across racial as well as gender lines, the index cards on which you note each new piece of information should be labeled under that *broad heading*, regardless of whether it comes from books, journals, newspapers, etc. If the material does not fit under that heading, but is important to your research subject, make a new heading.

The subject you finally chose for your American history paper is significantly more narrow than the general topic, "Women's Rights Movement" with which you began your research. Nevertheless, there is a great deal of material to read and assimilate. Index cards make this process easier. Writing down the important facts relating to your chosen topic, and filing each card carefully under selected broad headings as you go along, is a method by which large amounts of information become manageable and accessible when you begin to write. With practice, you will streamline and tailor this process and develop your own individual research style.

To sum up: each index card should contain a broad heading, a specific fact about your topic that relates to that heading, and the source from which you obtained it. The more you read, the more leads to new information you locate. Determine how important each new lead is to your subject. The categories and numbers of broad headings grow as you learn more about your topic. So does the pile of index cards.

Writing A Thesis Statement

After you have spent some time reading and taking notes, begin to think about the **thesis** of your paper. Unlike an encyclopedia entry, your paper should not be a simple recitation of facts. The goal in writing a college-level research paper is to use your acquired knowledge of the topic and your interpretations of the facts to introduce a theme, central idea, or argument in your paper: a *thesis*. This thesis should tell your audience – in this case, your professor – what proposition, theme, idea, or argument you plan to support with facts and interpretations in your paper. A thesis statement ought to be clear and definite, a precise as well as a concise expression of what you have created.

Faced with all the information that you have gathered, you may be somewhat uncertain about what your thesis statement should say. Refer once again to the sample topic; you might choose a thesis statement that reflects the division which existed between groups working for women's suffrage and those arguing for protection for African-Americans' voting rights. Such a thesis statement could read:

> During the last quarter of the nineteenth century a variety of different organizations worked to win suffrage for women and to guarantee it for African-Americans. These groups never united,

however, and each fought to achieve its own goals. A national move for universal enfranchisement never emerged.

This thesis statement informs your reader of the argument or position on the subject that you will present in your paper. Now it is up to you to gather solid evidence and organize it convincingly enough to demonstrate that you accurately support your thesis.

Outlining

With you thesis statement and your index cards at hand, you can begin to put together an **outline** that supports the argument you are asserting. At this point, those broad headings you created will be of great assistance. Take some time to look through the headings and think about how each one supports your thesis statement. If some seem irrelevant to your premise, set them aside. Do not throw them away; you may find that later on they have a place in your paper. Here are some likely broad headings for the sample topic:

- Women's groups who supported suffrage across racial as well as gender lines
- Women's groups who opposed voting rights for minorities
- Groups who supported African-Americans' voting rights and opposed women's suffrage
- Speeches by supporters of women's suffrage who opposed African-American rights
- Speeches by supporters of African-American rights who opposed women's suffrage
- Speeches by supporters of women's suffrage who advocated African-American suffrage

-Speeches by supporters of African-American rights
    who called for women's suffrage
  -Leaders of women's suffrage groups and their view
    of African-American rights
  -Leaders of African-American civil rights movements
    and their stands on women's suffrage
  -Fourteenth and Fifteenth Amendments – History of
    and Reaction to
  -Reconstruction and African-American voting
  -Success of Women's Suffrage – Brief History
  -Civil Rights Movement of 1960s – Final Success
  -Opposition to Women's Suffrage
  -Opposition to Voting Rights for African-Americans

These categories, and your thesis statement, serve as your guide in preparing your outline.

Outlining is an important step in the writing process. Preparing an outline forces you to consider the quality and quantity of the material you have collected. If you find that your outline is vague and short, ask yourself if you have enough information to write a paper. You will find that constructing an outline helps to clarify your thesis statement. It also points out where your weaknesses lie and directs you to areas where you need more research.

The length of your paper will determine how long and detailed your outline should be. If your assignment is relatively short, five pages or under, you must be careful to limit your topic so that you can adequately address it in such a brief paper. In this case, rather than discuss both groups, just focus on the women's suffrage movement in the nineteenth century:

I. Introduction
   A. Thesis statement
II. Background of Women's Suffrage Movement before the

Civil War
    A. Society of Friends
    B. Abolition Movement
    C. Seneca Falls Convention
III. Civil War and Reconstruction
    A. Failure of Fourteenth Amendment to include women
    B. Division within Women's Suffrage Movement over support for Fourteenth and Fifteenth Amendments
IV. Divisions within the Women's Suffrage Movement over tactics
    A. American Woman's Suffrage Association
    B. National Woman's Suffrage Association
V. Success at the state level
    A. Wyoming and other western states
    B. Municipal and local elections
VI. Conclusion
    A. Moving towards the 20th century

The following example is a detailed outline developed from the broad headings and thesis statement of a much longer paper on the women's movement:

I. Introduction
    A. Thesis statement
II. Historical background
    B. History of Women's Suffrage Movement before the Civil War
        1. Society of Friends
        2. Seneca Falls Convention
    C. History of voting rights for African-Americans in the 19th century
        1. Slavery in America
        2. Civil War

    3. Reconstruction
     a. Limitations on voting after emancipation
 III. Suffrage/voting rights efforts after the Civil War
   A. Groups who worked for women's suffrage
   B. Groups who advocated voting rights for African-Americans
 IV. Tensions between the two groups
   A. Attitudes of suffragists toward African-American rights
    1. Suffragists who supported African-American rights
     a. speeches of leaders
     b. public statements from groups
    2. Suffragists who opposed African-American rights
     a. speeches of leaders
     b. public statements from groups
   B. Attitudes of groups supporting African-American voting rights
    1. Groups who supported suffrage
     a. speeches of leaders
     b. public statements from groups
    2. Groups who opposed suffrage
     a. speeches of leaders
     b. public statements from groups
 V. Failure of both efforts during 19th century
   A. Success of "Jim Crow" laws in South
   B. Failure of Women's Suffrage
 VI. Inability of groups to coordinate and combine
   A. Divisions between the groups
   B. Societal limitations
 VII. Conclusion

  As you see, an outline enables you to take the broad headings from your note cards and begin to organize your thoughts into a logical argument. Outlines are not cast in stone. If you decide that some portion is unnecessary or that you need more information to flesh out your argument, alter your outline to reflect those changes at any time. Use your outline as a testing board; a topic that seems out of place in your outline will probably present similar problems in the body of your paper.

Writing Aids

There are three important books that every writer should have nearby before beginning to write. One is a **manual of style**. The appearance (format) of completed research papers, theses, and dissertations all must confom to a particular style. Manuals of style serve as a reference guide to help you prepare the form of your paper correctly. The names of several excellent ones appear later in this chapter.

The second book you need is a **dictionary**. Purchase the best dictionary that you can afford. Use it frequently. Computer spell-check capabilities have simplified the work of research writers; however, no machine can answer all the questions and problems with words and their usage that you will encounter as you write creatively.

A **thesaurus** is a dictionary of synonyms and antonyms. Synonyms are words that have the same or nearly the same meaning. The words, "friend," "pal," and "chum" are synonyms. Antonyms are words of opposite meaning, in this case, "enemy," "foe," and "adversary." A thesaurus helps you add variety to your choice of words without losing your meaning, and you avoid sounding repetitious.

Introductions and Conclusions

With thesis statement, outline, and organized index cards at hand, it is time to begin writing. A research paper, as with any essay, has three parts: **an introduction, a body, and a conclusion**.

Use your thesis statement in your *introduction*. Tell your reader what subject you are writing about and what point or points you are going to make about it. You may be tempted to use flowery or extravagant language in your introduction to impress your audience. Resist doing this. Your instructor has been at the process longer than you have. The grandest words in the language will not impress, nor will they disguise, a poorly researched paper. Keep the introduction crisp, simple, and straight-forward as you outline the issues you intend to address.

Conclusions, placed at the end of the paper, serve a similar purpose. A good conclusion draws together the various elements of the paper into a tight package. Include your thesis statement in this section as well. Unlike the introduction, however, where you proposed your thesis as an argument you intended to prove, here you remind your reader of the evidence you have presented.

In essence your introduction says, "here is what I have discovered. I intend to present facts that will support my discovery." Your conclusion states, "I provided you with these facts (very *briefly* restated). Based on the strength of this evidence, I have concluded that my thesis statement is true."

A strong *conclusion* includes notation of any flaws or questions that have arisen in your paper. Remember this: your purpose is not to mislead your audience but to inform them. If you realize that certain issues still remain unresolved, say so. Some of the most interesting and innovative historical scholarship comes from dialogues in journals between scholars who are examining related topics. We all have something to learn from one another. It is perfectly acceptable to acknowledge that you do not have all the answers.

The Body of the Paper

The introduction and conclusion are condensed restatements of the argument you are presenting. The **body of the paper** must contain the argument itself. Here your goal is to construct a succession of intelligent and orderly paragraphs.

Most paragraphs should contain a topic sentence that states the paragraph's central idea. The topic sentence identifies the issue that you will develop in the body of the paragraph. Following sentences should contribute to this central idea and to each other in a unified and coherent manner. You might include examples of the central idea or details to amplify and illustrate it more fully.

Identify a person by full name and title the first time you mention him or her. Subsequent references to that person should be with pronouns unless a second proper name intervenes and makes the pronoun's antecedent unclear.

At one time the use of the masculine pronouns, "he," "his," and "him," were used exclusively to include both sexes or either sex. Obviously, this has always been inaccurate, but efforts to correct the problem created new ones. Some writers use "him and her," or "he/she," which grows tedious both to write and to read after the first several times around. Others solve the problem by avoiding single pronouns altogether: "A person should...," or "Everyone wants...." The worst solution to the problem belongs to those writers who, in an effort to offend no one, constantly switch pronoun genders at random from male to female and back in their writing. This produces an unpleasant, dizzying effect on their readers, magnifying rather than curing the problem. There is as yet no good solution to this problem of how to embrace in writing both human genders equally. Until then, it is enough that you, as a writer, be sensitive to your audience and also be aware that half the people of the world are not described as "he," "his," and "him." Other than that, you are on your own here.

Each part of the paper must be clearly relevant to what precedes it and lead logically into the next section. The best way to assure this is to develop adequate **transitions**. Carefully thought-out transisitions are a key to creating a paper that flows smoothly. Transitions are paragraphs or sentences that wrap up the ideas you have discussed and introduce the next item to be considered. Beside acting as connectors, good transitions do more; they provide original analysis, tell your audience why you believe these two sections are related, and solidify your argument.

Consider our example. It will be necessary to write a transition between the sections on the history of women's suffrage and the history of the fight for African-American freedom before the Civil War. A transition between these two ideas might read:

> The individuals who were involved in the movement to extend suffrage to women recognized that there were others in American society who endured greater repression that did free white females. They were particularly distressed by the plight of African-American slaves, and in the decades before the Civil War, many of those who worked to allow women the right to vote joined with freed slaves, Quakers, and others to demand that slavery be outlawed in the United States.

In this transition you began by reminding the reader of the topic just discussed, the women's suffrage movement before the Civil War. From there, you moved to introduce the next subject, the demand for the end of slavery. Finally you showed the connection between the two. With the transition complete, you are prepared to write about the fight to end slavery.

Twelve Basic Rules For Good Writing

Here are some basic rules for good writing of historical

research papers.

1. Avoid the use of the first and second person (I and you).
2. Periods and commas always go within quotation marks.
3. Write complete sentences with subject, verb, and object. Do not use unnecessary adjectives and adverbs.
4. Never use contractions or abbreviations.
5. Avoid the use of the word "feel," if what you mean is "think" or "say."
6. Do not split infinitives. "To boldly go" is a split infinitive. Correctly stated, it is "to go boldly" or "boldly to go."
7. Avoid the use of slang or jargon.
8. Make certain that single subjects have single verbs, plural subjects, plural verbs.
9. Break a long sentence into two or even three shorter ones.
10. Use active verbs. The English language has more verbs than any other, so take advantage of them. Choose, select, elect, opt, pick, cull, prefer, hand-pick, single-out a variety of them as you write; they will improve, better, help, benefit, enhance your paper.
11. Avoid the passive voice at all times. In the active voice, the subject does something. "A dog barked somewhere." "The boy opens the door." Active voice sentences are precise and direct. In the passive voice, the subject receives the action of the verb. "Somewhere a bark was made by a dog." "The door is opened by the boy." The

passive voice makes sentences sound wordy and muddy.
12. Say it simply and strive for economy.
Unnecessary words and phrases clutter an otherwise well-researched paper. Examine each sentence individually. Determine that each word adds something necessary for meaning and clarity. Eliminate those that do not.

Using Other's Work: Do's And Don'ts

Webster's Ninth New Collegiate Dictionary defines "to plagiarize" as: to steal and pass off (the ideas or words of another) as one's own; use (a creative production) without crediting the source; to commit literary theft; to present as new and original an idea or product derived from an existing source.[1]

When you write any sort of academic research paper, it is necessary to rely upon the work of others. There is nothing wrong in doing this, so long as you understand and follow the rules that govern this practice. In preparing a research paper, *you must never plagiarize*, that is, *portray someone else's work as your own original thought*. The penalties for academic plagiarism are severe; at some universities you may be forced to withdraw from school if you are caught and convicted. It is essential that your work be original. Some students believe that if they do not copy the exact words, they have not committed plagiarism. That is not the case; if you have represented someone else's thoughts or ideas as your own, you have stolen them.

The following is a direct quote from a book by Eric Foner called *Reconstruction: America's Unfinished Revolution 1863-1877*. Read it carefully and notice the three facts that he presents in this passage.

> With black's enfranchisement, "women remained the only class of citizens wholly unrepresented in the government." And despite the disintegration of the abolitionist-feminist alliance in disputes over the post-war [Fourteenth and Fifteenth] amendments, a broadly based, independent movement continued to demand an end to the restrictions on women's social and legal rights.[2]

To **paraphrase** means to restate a source. The following, Paraphrase A, is incorrect and constitutes plagiarism of Foner's work.

> When blacks got enfranchised, women were the only citizens who could not vote. Their abolitionist-feminist alliance fell apart due to disputes over the post-war amendments, but an independent movement formed to demand the end to the restrictions on women's rights.

Notice here how closely Paraphrase A follows the original, using many phrases word for word. If you write it in this form in your research paper, and present it as your own work, then you have plagiarized Foner's work.

Paraphrase B is an example of correct usage of the three facts contained in Foner's statement.

> The abolitionist-feminist alliance broke apart when the post-war amendments gave the vote to blacks and not to women. However, the struggle for women's social and legal rights continued.

Paraphrase B contains the three main points but does not copy the phrases of the original paragraph. Using essential facts of research materials, but in your own words, does not constitute plagiarism.

Manuals Of Style

There are legitimate ways to utilize information from other writers, so long as you appropriately indicate (**cite**) the source of the material you are using. Acceptable citation models are found in **manuals of style**. Four commonly used are: *A Manual for Writers of Term Papers, Theses, and Dissertations*, by Kate L. Turabian, *The Harbrace College Handbook*, *The MLA Handbook for Writers of Research Papers*, and *The Chicago Manual of Style for Authors, Editors, and Copywriters*. These books are important guides and any of them is worth purchasing. It is helpful to ask which guide your instructor prefers that you follow.

Footnotes And Endnotes

The above-mentioned manuals teach you how to write **footnotes** or **endnotes** and a **bibliography**. *Footnotes* or *endnotes* are the **citations** within the text that identify the sources of the information, ideas, opinions, and interpretations that you have used in your paper. Footnotes, on the bottom of the page on which such information appears, are quickly available to the reader. Endnotes, placed either at the end of each chapter or all together at the back of the paper or book, require more time to locate. However, either method of citation is acceptable. Both footnotes and endnotes are indicated in the text by slightly-elevated small numbers placed immediately after the information you have gathered from another author's work.

Consider once more the sample index card from the paper on the women's movement found earlier in this chapter. You might utilize the information on that card in this manner when writing your paper:

> In Chicago in 1896 the suffrage group, Sorosis, demanded "universal suffrage and equal rights for all the people."[1]

Your citation of this quote in the footnote or endnote will appear as follows:

> [1]Steven M. Buechler, *The Transformation of the Woman Suffrage Movement* (New Brunswick: Rutgers UP, 1986), 69.

This footnote form is based on *The MLA Handbook for Writers of Research Papers*. It contains all the information necessary to enable a reader to go directly to this book and find the original source. The data inside the parentheses indicates the place of publication, the institution that published the book, and the year of publication. The final number is the page number from which the information was drawn. All footnotes and endnotes, no matter which manual you rely on, will include these facts.

The correct form of a citation is a requirement for a research paper, not merely a capricious suggestion. Be certain to copy the form *exactly*: periods, commas, colons, parentheses, etc., for every footnote or endnote. There are differences between citations for a book and a scholarly journal. The manual of style that you are using will be an invaluable help in this task.

Bibliography

Footnotes alone are not enough to provide your readers with access to all the information that you have used to put together your paper. Frequently, you may rely heavily on a source that you may never actually cite in the body of your text. Ensure that all the materials you have used are given appropriate credit by attaching a **bibliography** to the end of your paper. A bibliography is an alphabetized list of all the publications and sources that you have referred to, studied, examined, in researching your paper. The same manuals that provide formats for footnotes will be useful in putting together your bibliography. Unfortunately, the form is slightly different for bibliographies than for foot or endnotes, and it, too, must be done as exactly.

The following entry will include the book, *The Transformation of the Woman Suffrage Movement*, in your bibliography. Remember that bibliographies are alphabetized by the author's last name.

>Buechler, Steven M. *The Transformation of the Woman Suffrage Movement.* New Brunswick: Rutgers UP, 1986.

The primary differences between bibliographic entries and footnotes lie in the use of periods in the bibliography and placement of the author's last name at the beginning of the bibliographical citation.

Choosing A Title

An appropriate **title** fits the subject of the paper. The thesis statement may or may not contain some possible titles. It is a good place to look first. You might call your American history paper, "The Failure of Universal Enfranchisement of Women and African-Americans in the Nineteenth Century," or perhaps, "Woman Suffrage and Voting Rights for African-Americans in the Post Civil War Period." You may use dates in your title or ask a rhetorical question, that is, a question asked but with no answer expected. "Who Can Vote? Minority Citizens and the Right to Vote, 1865-1890." The possibilities are as endless as your imagination. However, attempt to make the title as encompassing of your subject as possible.

First Drafts

One of the best ways to improve on the quality of your final paper is to write a **first draft**. A draft will help you in several ways. Set a personal deadline several days or a week before the class deadline. This will guarantee that you have your paper completed when it is due. Finishing ahead of the due date gives you a period of time to distance yourself from your paper before you proofread. If you have just spent ten days writing in front of the computer, it is very difficult to see the flaws in your work. Time away from your first draft will permit you to be objective when you return to it.

The next step is to **proofread** your paper carefully. Read it out loud several times. Hearing it, as well as reading it, will help you locate any grammatical flaws. Look for spelling and stylistic errors. Have you been consistent in your use of tenses? Do your transitions carry the reader from one section to the next? Is your argument strong and have you proven your case? Some part may profit from a complete rewrite. Set aside your reluctance and do it.

No matter how well done your paper is, or how proud of it you are, there are still ways to improve it. Computers have simplified the process of rewriting a great deal, for you can turn a rough draft into a finished copy right on your computer screen. Take this last opportunity to give your paper a final polish. The end results definitely will reflect the attention to detail and the care that you have given to your paper. Conversely, should you fail to do so, the paper you turn in will reflect this also. There is no substitute for your best.

PART TWO – TAKING NOTES IN CLASS AND PREPARING FOR EXAMINATIONS

Taking Notes In Class

History classes are taught by lecture. Instructors emphasize in lectures the information that they consider important for you to know. There is no way to remember all the important points of a lecture without taking notes. The notes that you take during lectures are your study material. Inattention and failure on your part to take adequate notes means that when exam time arrives, you have no way to retrieve this essential material for study.

Systematic, organized note-taking is a skill you can learn. One good method is to draw a line down the center of your notebook paper. As you read your assigned text before class, take notes from the book on one side of the line. In class write the notes from the instructor's lecture on the other side. Your notes reflect both the book and the lecture on information covered that day. Also, try taking a minute after class to underline the lesson's important points in your lecture notes. With practice, you will develop for yourself a method that helps you to best deal with a large body of information in a way most helpful for you.

Writing In Class Assignments

Class writing assignments are most frequently essay tests, short answer questions, and identifications. Writing a research paper is different from writing exercises that must be completed in class. However some of the suggestions you have just read will help you prepare for examinations of this kind.

Essay Examinations

The approach of an essay examination is one of the most frightening events in a college student's life. You will achieve success only through thorough preparation. If your instructor has given you study questions, make use of them. Read each question carefully, making certain that you understand the type of response it is seeking. After you have examined the question, go to your textbook and locate that topic. Ideally, you have already read the book and have gained some general information. To prepare for the exam, you need to study both your book and your class notes.

The best way to bring together information from the textbook and from class notes is to outline. Using your book and your notes, prepare an outline similar in form to the example that appears earlier in this chapter. Think of your essay as a mini-research paper. Your book and class lectures provide the research notes from which you must prepare that paper. You may not be able to memorize all the outlines you prepare for the exam, but the intensive study process you follow in preparing them will assure you an excellent review of all materials.

Even if your professor has not given you study questions, you still can use this process to prepare for a test. In all probability your lecture notes follow the same general outline as your textbook. Take time to match your notes with the appropriate sections in your text. Your notes will relate to the textbook either chronologically or topically. Study them together as a unit. You may not have time to write extensive outlines for each section, but at least formulate a broad summary of each topic. Ask yourself the question, "If I had to write an essay about this, do I know enough to do it?"

When you begin your exam, *read* each question carefully. Underline all the points your instructor has asked you to address. Tailor your responses accordingly. Sometimes students who are really well-prepared impetuously begin to write when they see a few key words. They may know a great deal about the topic, yet never answer the question because they did not read it fully. The results are as sad as if they had failed to study at all.

As with a research paper, an essay has an introduction, a body, and a conclusion. Obviously, you are limited in both space and time in writing an essay. Write as concise an introduction as you can, making certain that you state your thesis. Fill the body of your essay with as many facts as you can muster to support your answer. Draw everything together in your conclusion. Before you hand in your paper, re-read the points that you underlined on each question to make sure you have answered them all.

To avoid running out of time, plan ahead how long you can afford to spend on each question. Take a watch and follow your time plan as closely as possible. If you are pressed for time, you may need to reduce the conclusion to one sentence. If it is evident that you are not going to be able to complete your essay, you might outline the last few paragraphs of your answer rather than leaving your answer unfinished. You will not get full credit for this, but at least it tells your professor that you know the material.

Short Answers And Identifications

Short answer questions on an exam indicate whether or not you have studied your assigned materials. Unlike essay questions, short answer exams require little writing but a great deal of information in a small amount of space.

Your professors will indicate in what form they expect your responses to the questions to be. Perhaps it is just a word or a phrase. However, unless instructed otherwise, be prepared to write your answers in full sentence form.

Read each question carefully. When answering short answer questions, be absolutely certain that you provide the correct response. With these more precise questions there is less room for error.

Identification questions are much like short answer questions. Here you respond, not to a question, but to a phrase or word, a limited topic. To fully describe a term, remember the five "Ws" – who, what, where, when, and why. Who are the people involved in this topic? What are the elements or events that make up this subject? Where did these things take place? When did this incident occur, or when did this person live? Why are they important to historians? If you fully answer these questions, you are on the way to writing a complete identification.

Miscellaneous Test Taking Suggestions

Many history tests include sections of multiple choice questions, fill-in-the-blanks, matching, and true-false questions. There is little writing involved here but they are integrally related to the written segments of your test. It is frequently to your advantage to answer these portions of the test first. They may provide information that will aid you in writing the essay portions.

Conclusion

Writing for a history course is a manageable task; it should not be an intimidating or oppressive obstacle. Remember, in both your research and your writing, be systematic and orderly. When building an argument, make sure that each element logically supports your case. Do not take credit for someone else's work; be extremely careful about citing sources. Be consistent in preparing footnotes or endnotes and bibliography. There is no excuse for sloppiness in any part of your paper. Invest in a recognized manual of style, dictionary, and thesaurus. They are worthwhile expenditures. Finally, be fair to yourself and respectful of your ability. Accept the fact that you have to commit effort and time in preparation for history classes. When you do your best, the rewards you receive in the long run will outweigh the effort and energy you expend.

ENDNOTES

[1] *Webster's Ninth new Collegiate Dictionary* (1990), s.v. "plagiarize."

[2] Eric Foner, *Reconstruction: America's Unfinished Revolution 1863-1877* (New York: Harper & Row, 1988)..

CHAPTER FOUR

BASIC BIBLIOGRAPHY

This basic bibliography is a brief list of history books available in many college libraries. Selected to help you begin your study and research, its use does not take the place of a thorough investigation of specialized bibliographies and the library's card catalog. There are several kinds of works listed under the subject headings: first are research guides – bibliographies and other books containing research helps for particular periods and subjects. Next are a list of books written about the specific historical times and topics.

Do not overlook the possibility that useful material may be located under several subject headings. For example to find books dealing with the African-American experience in the Americas the subject headings *Africa, African-American, American Women, West Virginia, Colonial, Nineteenth,* and *Twentieth Century United States* all contain books that address this subject. The books are listed with the author's name first, title of the book, and date of publication.

ANCIENT HISTORY
Research Guides:
Walbank, Frank. *Studies in Greek and Roman History and Historiography.* 1985.
Yonah, Michael and Israel Shatzman, eds. *Illustrated Encyclopedia of the Classical World.* 1975.

Books:
Beard, Mary and Michael Crawford. *Rome in the Late Republic.* 1985.

Boardman, John, Jasper Griffin, and Oswyn Murray. *Greece and the Hellenistic World.* 1988.

Bowerstock, G.W. *Augustus and the Greek World.* 1965.

The Cambridge Ancient History. 1989.

Finley, M.I.. *Ancient Greeks.* 1963.

Forrest, W.G. *The Emergence of Greek Democracy.* 1966.

Garnsey, Peter and Richard Saller. *The Roman Empire: Economy Society and Culture.* 1987.

Knapp, A. Bernard. *The History and Culture of Ancient Western Asia and Egypt.* 1987.

Kramer, Samuel N. *History Begins at Sumar.* 1981.

Stair, Chester. *Ancient Romans.* 1971

MEDIEVAL EUROPE
Research Guides:
Boyce, G.C. *Literature of Medieval History.* 1980.

Paetow, L.J. *A Guide to the Study of Medieval History.* 1980.

Books:
Baldwin, John. *The Scholastic Culture of the Middle Ages.* 1971.

Benson, Robert and Giles Constable, eds. *Renaissance and Renewal in the Twelfth Century.* 1982.

Collis, Louise. *Memoirs of a Medieval Woman: The Life and Times of Margery Kempe.* 1983.

Duby, Georges. *The Early Growth of the European Economy: Warriors and Peasants from the Seventh to the Twelfth Century.* 1974.

James, Edward. *The Franks.* 1988.

Herlihy, David. *Medieval Households.* 1985.

Huizinga, Johann. *The Waning of the Middle Ages.* 1924.

Lopez, Robert S. *The Commercial Revolution of the Middle Ages.* 1971.

Pirenne, Henri. *Mohammed and Charlemagne.* 1955.

White, Lynn. *Medieval Technology and Social Change*. 1964.

CELTS AND VIKINGS
Research Guides:
Hector, Michael. *Internal Colonialism: The Celtic Fringe in British National Development 1536-1966*. 1975.
Nordstrom, Byron, ed. *Dictionary of Scandinavian History*. 1986.

Books:
Almgren, Bertil, et al. *The Viking: The Settlers, Ships, Swords, and Sagas of the Nordic Age*. 1991.
Crossley-Holland, Kevin. *The Norse Myths*. 1980.
Delaney, Frank. *Legends of the Celts*. 1992.
Ellis, Peter Berresford. *The Celtic Empire: The First Millennium of Celtic History, 1000 BC - 51 AD*. 1990.
Jesch, Judith. *Women in the Viking Age*. 1991.
Jones, Gwyn. *A History of the Vikings*. 1984.
Logan, F. Donald. *The Vikings in History*. 1983.
Matthews, Caitlin. *The Elements of the Celtic Tradition*. 1991.
Matthews, John, comp. *A Celtic Reader: Selections from Celtic Legend, Scholarship, and Story*. 1992.
Markale, Jean. *Women of the Celts*. 1986.

RENAISSANCE AND REFORMATION EUROPE
Research Guides:
Kohl, Benjamin, ed. *Renaissance Humanism 1300-1550: A Bibliography of Materials in English*. 1985.
Ozment, Steven. *Reformation Europe: A Guide to Research*. 1982.

Books:
Davis, Natalie Z. *Society and Culture in Early Modern France*. 1975.
Debus, Allen G. *Man and Nature in the Renaissance*. 1978.

Dickens, A.J. *The English Reformation*. 2d ed. 1989.
Dunn, Richard. *The Age of Religious Wars, 1559-1715*. 1970.
Hillerbrand, Hans, ed. *The Reformation*. 1987.
Huppert, George. *After the Black Death: A Social History of Early Modern Europe*. 1986.
King, Margaret L. *Women of the Renaissance*. 1991.
Koenigsberger, H.S., George Mosse, and E.C. Bowler. *Europe in the Sixteenth Century*. 1989.
Kohl, Benjamin and Ronald Witt, eds. *The Earthly Republics: Italian Humanists on Government and Society*. 1978.
Kristeller, Paul. *Renaissance Thought*. 1955.
Martines, Lauro. *Power and Imagination: City-States in Renaissance Italy*. 1979.
Rice, Eugene Jr. *Foundations of Modern Europe*. 1970.
Waley, Daniel. *Italian City Republics*. 1969.

ASIA
Research Guides:
Asia: A Selected and Annotated Guide to Reference Works. 1971.
Bibliography of Asian Studies. Published annually.

Books:
Burki, Shahid. *Pakistan: A Nation in the Making*. 1986.
Embee, Ainslie T., ed. *Encyclopedia of Asian History*. 4 vols. 1988.
Fairbank, John K., Edwin O. Reischauer, and Albert M. Craig. *East Asia: Tradition and Transformation*. 1989.
Hunter, Janet E. *The Emergence of Modern Japan: An Introductory History Since 1853*. 1989.
Kodansha Encyclopedia of Japan. 8 vols. 1983.
Livingston, William and William Louis, eds. *Australia, New Zealand, and the Pacific Islands Since the First World War*. 1979.
The Oxford History of Modern India, 1740-1975. 1978.

Pye, Lucian W. *China: An Introduction*. 1991.
Reischauer, Edwin. *Japan: Story of a Nation*. 1964.
Romein, Jan. *An Asian Century: A History of Modern Nationalism in Asia*. 1962.
Schirokauer, Conrad. *A Brief History of Chinese Civilization*. 1991.
Twitchett, Denis and John L. Fairbank, eds. *The Cambridge History of China*. 14 vols. 1978-.

AFRICA/THE MIDDLE EAST
Research Guides:
Paden, John and Edward Soja, eds. *The African Experience*. 1970.
Simon, Reeva. *The Modern Middle East: A Guide to Reference Tools in the Social Sciences*. 1978.
Wise, Kenda, comp. *Africa: Selected References*. 1990.

Books:
Ajayi, J.F.A. and M. Crowder. *History of West Africa*. 1976.
The Cambridge History of Africa. 1975.
Diop, Cheikh Anta. *The African Origins of Civilization: Myth or Reality?* 1974.
Freund, Bill. *The Making of Contemporary Africa*. 1984.
July, Robert W. *A History of the African People*. 1980.
Ogot, B.A., ed. *Zamani*. 1974.
Perry, Glenn. *The Middle East: 14 Islamic Centuries*. 1983.
Rodney, Walter. *How Europe Underdeveloped Africa*. 1972.
Sabini, John. *Islam: A Primer*. 1983.
Sachar, Howard. *A History of Israel*. Vol I, 1976, vol. II, 1987.
Wilson, Monica, ed. *The Oxford History of South Africa*. 2 vols. 1979.

RUSSIA/SOVIET UNION/SUCCESSOR STATES
Research Guides:
ABSEES (American Bibliography of Soviet and East European Studies).

Books in English on the Soviet Union 1917-1973: A Bibliography. 1975.

Books:
Chamberlin, W.H. *The Russian Revolution.* 2 vols. 1965.
Colton, Timothy and Robert Legvold, eds. *After the Soviet Union.* 1992.
Cracraft, James, ed. *Peter the Great Transforms Russia.* 1991.
Daniels, Robert, ed. *The Stalin Revolution.* 1972.
Doder, Dusko. *Heretic in the Kremlin.* 1991.
Dukes, Paul. *The Making of Russian Absolutism 1613-1801.* 1982.
Edmonds, Robin. *Soviet Foreign Policy: The Paradox of Super Power.* 1975.
Gati, Charles. *The Bloc That Failed: Soviet-East European Relations in Transition.* 1990.
Medvedev, Roy and Zhores. *Khrushechev: The Years in Power.* 1976.
Pomper, Philip. *The Russian Revolutionary Intelligentsiia.* 1986.

EAST/CENTRAL EUROPE
Research Guides:
Horak, Stephan. *Junior Slavica: A Selected Annotated Bibliography of Books in English on Russia and Eastern Europe.* 1968.
Magocsi, Paul. *Carpatho-Rusyn Studies: An Annotated Bibliography.* 1988.

Books:
Brown, J.F. *Surge to Freedom: The End of Communist Rule in Eastern Europe.* 1991.
Carsten, F.L. *Origins of Prussia.* 1954.
Davies, Norman. *Heart of Europe: A Short History of Poland.* 1984.
Glenny, Misha. *The Rebirth of History: Eastern Europe in the Age of Democracy.* 1990.
Jelavich, C. and B., eds. *The Balkans in Transition.* 1963.

Kann, Robert. *The Multinational Empire: Nationalism and National Reform in the Habsburg Monarchy, 1848-1918*. 1950.

Kobel, Joseph. *Twentieth Century Czechoslovakia: The Meaning of Its History*. 1977.

Kovrig, Bennett. *Of Walls and Bridges: The United States and Eastern Europe*. 1991.

Macartney, C.A., ed. *The Habsburg and Hohenzollern Dynasties in the Seventeenth and Eighteenth Centuries*. 1970.

——. *Hungary: A Short History*. 1962.

Pagès, Georges. *The Thirty Year War 1619-1648*. 1970.

Ramet, Sabrina. *Social Currents in Eastern Europe: The Sources and Meaning of the Great Transformation*. 1991.

Rothschild, Joseph. *East Central Europe Between the Two Wars*. 1974.

——. *Return to Diversity: A Political History of East Central Europe Since 1945*. 1988.

Stokes, Gale, ed. *From Stalinism to Pluralism: A Documentary History of Eastern Europe Since 1945*. 1991.

GERMANY
Research Guides:
ABC-Clio. *The Weimar Republic: A Historical Bibliography*. 1984.

ABC-Clio. *The Third Reich, 1933-1919, A Historical Bibliography*. 1984.

Books:
Barraclough, Geoffrey. *The Origins of Modern Germany*. 1963.

Bismarck, Otto von. *Memoirs*. 2 vols. 1966.

Bracher, Karl Dietrich. *The German Dictatorship*. 1970.

Bullock, Alan. *Hitler: A Study in Tyranny*. 1971.

Craig, Gordon. *Germany: 1855-1915*. 1978.

Eyck, Frank. *Frankfurt Parliament 1848-1849*. 1968.

Frevert, Ute. *Women in German History: From Bourgeois*

Emancipation to Sexual Liberation. 1989.
Fritsch-Bournazel, Renata. *Europe and German Reunification.* 1992.
Golay, John Ford. *The Founding of the Federal Republic of Germany.* 1958.
Hilberg, Raul. *The Destruction of European Jewry.* 1961.
Koch, H.W. *A Constitutional History of Germany in the Nineteenth and Twentieth Centuries.* 1984.
Stephenson, Jill. *Nazi Organisation of Women.* 1981.
Stolper, Gustav, et al. *The German Economy, 1870 to the Present.* 1967.

MODERN EUROPE
Research Guides:
Cook, Chris. *The Longman Handbook of Modern European History 1763-1985.* 1987.
Davies, Alun, comp. *Modern European History, 1494-1789.* 1966.

Books:
The Cambridge Economic History of Europe. 7 vols.
Carr, Raymond. *Spain 1808-1939.* 1966.
Cobban, Alfred. *In Search of Humanity: The Role of the Enlightenment in Modern History.* 1960.
Cook, Don. *Forging the Alliance: NATO 1945-1950.* 1989.
Doyle, William. *The Old European Order: 1660-1800.* 1978.
Dziewanowski, M.K. *War at Any Price: World War II in Europe 1939-1948.* 1987.
Geddis, John Lewis. *The Long Peace: Inquiries into the History of the Cold War.* 1987.
Gildea, Robert. *Barricades and Borders: Europe 1800-1914.* 1987.
Kissinger, Henry A. *A World Restored: Europe After Napoleon: Politics of Conservatism in a Revolutionary Age.* 1964.
Kossman, E.H. *The Low Countries: 1780-1940.* 1978.

Lee, W.R., ed. *European Demography and Economic Growth*. 1979.
Mack Smith, Denis. *Italy: A Modern History*. 1969.
Palmer, R.R. *History of the Modern World*. 1971.
Ridley, E.A. *Industrial Growth and Population Change*. 1961.
Ringer, Fritz. *Education and Society in Modern Europe*. 1979.
Robertson, Priscilla. *Revolutions of 1848*. 1952.
Taylor, A.J.P. *The Struggle for Mastery in Europe, 1845-1918*. 1965.
Wright, Gordon. *Ordeal of Total War, 1939-1945*. 1968.

EUROPEAN WOMEN
Research Guides:
Kelly, Joan, et al. *Bibliography in the History of European Women*. 1982.

Frey, Linda, Marsha Frey, and Joanne Schneider. *Women in Western European History: A Select Chronological, Geographical, and Topical Bibliography*. 1982.

Books:
Anderson, Bonnie S. and Judith P. Zinsser. *A History of Their Own*. 1988.

Bridenthal, Renata and Claudia Koonz. *Becoming Visible: Women in European History*. 1977.

Daly, Mary. *The Church and the Second Sex*. 1968.

Fraser, Antonia. *The Warrior Queens: The Legends and Lives of the Women Who Have Led Their Nations in War*. 1988.

Hill, Bridget. *Eighteenth Century Women: An Anthology*. 1987.

Lerner, Gerda. *The Creation of Patriarchy*. 1987.

Osborne, Martha Lee, ed. *Woman in Western Thought*. 1979.

Pomeroy, Sarah. *Goddesses, Whores, Wives, and Slaves: Women in Classical Antiquity*. 1975.

Poston, Carol H., ed. *Mary Wollstonecraft: A Vindication of the Rights of Woman [1792]: An Authoritative Text, Backgrounds, Criticism.*

1975.

Robertson, Priscilla. *An Experience of Women: Pattern and Change in Nineteenth Century Europe.* 1952.

Scott, Joan. *Gender and the Politics of History.* 1988.

Woolf, Virginia. *A Room of One's Own.* 1957.

GREAT BRITAIN
Research Guides:

Christie, Ian, comp. *British History Since 1760.* 1970.

Miller, Helen and Aubrey Newman, comps. *Early Modern British History, 1485-1760.* 1970.

Books:

Elton, G.R. *England Under the Tudors.* 3rd ed. 1992.

Hill, Christopher. *The Century of Revolution, 1603-1714.* 1961.

Hirst, Derek. *Authority and Conflict: England 1603-1658.* 1986.

Lander, J.R. *Government and Community: England 1450-1509.* 1980.

Lloyd, T.O. *The British Empire 1558-1983.* 1984.

McKenzie, R.T. *British Political Parties.* 1963.

Morgan, Kenneth O., ed. *The Oxford History of Britain.* 1984.

Morgan, Kenneth O. *The People's Peace: British History 1945-1988.* 1988.

Pollard, A.J. *The Wars of the Roses.* 1988.

Stenton, Frank M. *Anglo-Saxon England.* 1989.

Taylor, A.J.P. *English History 1914-1945.* 1965.

FRANCE
Research Guides:

Bowditch, John. *A Selected Bibliography on Modern French History 1600 to Present.* 1974.

Lough, John. *An Introduction to Seventeenth Century France.* 1961.

Books:

Clapham, J.H. *The Economic Development of Germany and France 1815-1914*. 1936.

Lacouture, Jean. *DeGaulle*. 1990.

Lefebvre, George. *The Coming of the French Revolution*. 1947.

Lewis, W.H. *The Splendid Century: Life in the France of Louis XIV*. 1953.

Markham, Felix. *Napoleon and the Awakening of Europe*. 1965.

Paxton, Robert. *Vichy France: Old Guard and New Order, 1940-1944*. 1972.

Power, Thomas. *Jules Ferry and the Renaissance of French Imperialism*. 1977.

Rioux, Jean Pierre. *The Fourth Republic 1944-1958*. 1987.

Scherman, Katherine. *The Birth of France: Warriors, Bishops, and Long-Haired Kings*. 1987.

Tapié, Victor L. *France in the Age of Louis XIII and Richelieu*. 1984.

Williams, Stuart, ed. *Socialism in France: From Jaures to Mitterand*. 1983.

Zelden, Theodore. *France 1848-1945*. 1973.

COLONIAL AMERICA
Research Guides:

Ammerman, Philip L. and Philip D. Morgan, eds. *Books About Early America*. 1989.

Greene, Jack P., ed. *The American Colonies in the Eighteenth Century*. 1969.

Books:

Axtell, James. *Beyond 1492: Encounters in Colonial North America*. 1992.

Countryman, Edward. *The American Revolution*. 1985.

Demos, John. *A Little Commonwealth*. 1988.

Jennings, Francis. *The Invasion of America: Indians, Colonialism, and *the Cant of Conquest.* 1975.

Jensen, Merrill. *The Making of the American Constitution.* 1958.

Maier, Pauline. *The Old Revolutionaries: Political Lives in the Age of Samuel Adams.* 1980.

Morgan, Edmund S. *American Slavery American Freedom.* 1975.

Perry, J.H. *The Establishment of the European Hegemony: 1415-1715.* 1959.

Ramsey, David. *The History of the American Revolution.* 1990.

Ulrich, Laurel Thatcher. *Good Wives: Image and Reality of the Lives of Women in Northern New England 1650-1750.* 1982.

NINETEENTH CENTURY UNITED STATES
Research Guides:

Basler, Roy P., et al, comp. *A Guide to Study of the United States of America: Representative Books Reflecting the Development of American Life and Thought.* 1960.

Moebs, Thomas, comp. *U.S. Reference-iana (1481-1899).* 1989.

Books:

Benedict, Michael. *Impeachment of Andrew Johnson.* 1973.

Bodner, John. *The Transplanted: The History of Immigrants in Urban America.* 1985.

Catton, Bruce. *The Centennial History of the Civil War.* 3 vols. 1961-1965.

Cunningham, Noble. *In Pursuit of Reason: The Life of Thomas Jefferson.* 1987.

McPherson, James. *Abraham Lincoln and the Second American Revolution.* 1991.

——. *Ordeal by Fire: The Civil War and Reconstruction.* 1982.

Rawley, James. *Race and Politics: "Bleeding Kansas" and the Coming of the Civil War.* 1969.

Roland, Charles. *American Iliad: The Story of the Civil War.* 1991.

Stampp, Kenneth. *The Peculiar Institution: Slavery in the Ante-bellum South*. 1956.

Ward, John William. *Andrew Jackson: Symbol for an Age*. 1955.

TWENTIETH CENTURY UNITED STATES
Research Guides:

Kaplan, Louis. *A Bibliography of American Autobiographies*. 1962.

Tingley, Donald F. *Social History of the United States: A Guide to Information Sources*. 1979.

Books:

Allen, Frederick Lewis. *Only Yesterday*. 1964.

Blum, John Morton. *V Was for Victory: Politics and American Culture During World War II*. 1976.

Brody, David. *Workers in Industrial America*. 1980.

Carter, Paul A. *The Twenties in America*. 1968.

Conklin, Paul. *The New Deal*. 1967.

Harris, William H. *The Harder We Run: Black Workers Since the Civil War*. 1982.

Link, Arthur S. and Richard L. McCormick. *Progressivism*. 1983.

McElvaine, Robert. *The Great Depression: America, 1929-1941*. 1984.

Porter, Glenn. *The Rise of Big Business, 1860-1920*. 1973.

Wiebe, Robert. *The Search for Order, 1967*. 1967.

UNITED STATES DIPLOMATIC HISTORY
Research Guides:

Burns, Richard, ed. *Guide to American Foreign Relations Since 1700*. 1983.

Goehlert, Robert. *Department of State and American Diplomacy: A Bibliography*. 1986.

Books:

Ambrose, Stephen. *Rise to Globalism: American Foreign Policy Since*

1938. 1983.

Chafe, William H. *The Unfinished Journey: America Since World War II*. 1968.

Dellek, Robert. *Franklin D. Roosevelt and the Origins of the Cold War 1932-1945*. 1979.

Herring, George. *America's Longest War*. 1986.

LeFeber, Walter. *America, Russia, and the Cold War*. 1985.

Levin, N. Gordon. *Woodrow Wilson and World Politics*. 1968.

Sherman, Martin J. *A World Destroyed: The Atomic Bomb and the Grand Alliance*. 1975.

Smith, Gaddis. *American Diplomacy During the Second World War*. 1965.

Wilson, John Huff. *American Business and Foreign Policy 1920-1933*. 1971.

AMERICAN WOMEN
Research Guides:

Common Women Collective. *Women in U.S. History: An Annotated Bibliography*. 1976.

Tingley, Elizabeth and Donald F. *Women and Feminism in American History: A Guide to Information Sources*. 1981.

Books:

Chafe, William. *Women and Equality: Changing Patterns in American Culture*. 1977.

Davies, Miranda and Ana Mariá Portugal, comp. *The Latin American Women's Movement: Reflections and Actions*. 1986.

Dubois, Ellen Carol and Vicki L. Ruiz, eds. *Unequal Sisters: A Multicultural Reader in U.S. Women's History*. 1990.

Engle, Paul. *Women in the American Revolution*. 1976.

Evans, Sara M. *Born for Liberty: A History of Women in America*. 1989.

Giddings, Paula. *When and Where I Enter: The Impact of Black Women on Race and Sex in America*. 1964.

Kessler-Harris, Alice. *Women Have Always Worked*. 1981.

Morgan, Edmund. *The Puritan Family*. 1952.

Trigger, Bruce. *The Huron: Farmers of the North*. 1990.

Ware, Susan, ed. *Modern American Women: A Documentary History*. 1969.

AFRICAN-AMERICAN HISTORY
Research Guides:
Davis, Nathaniel. *Afro-American Reference: An Annotated Bibliography of Selected Resources*. 1985.

Stevenson, Rosemary. *Index to Afro-American Reference Resources*. 1988.

Books:
Asante, Molefi. *Kemet, Afrocentricity and Knowledge*. 1990.

Bennett, Lerone. *Before the Mayflower: A History of Black America*. 1984.

Chejne, Anwar. *Muslim Spain: Its History and Culture*. 1974.

Dubois, W.E.B. *The Souls of Black Folk*. 1982.

Lane-Poole, Stanley. *The Story of the Moors in Spain*. 1990.

Proctor, Evelyn. *Alfonso X of Castile*. 1980.

Rogers, J.A. *From "Superman" to Man*. 1980.

Van Sertima, Ivan, ed. *The Golden Age of the Moor*. 1992.

White, Deborah Gray. *Ain't I a Woman?: Female Slaves in the Plantation South*. 1985.

Woodson, Carter G. *The Mis-Education of the Negro*. 1933.

WEST VIRGINIA HISTORY
Resource Guides:
Clagg, Samuel. *West Virginia Almanac*. 1975.

Vexler, Robert. *Chronicle and Document Handbook of the State of*

West Virginia. 1979.

Books:

Ambler, Charles. *Sectionalism in Virginia from 1776-1861.* 1910.

Cherniack, Martin. *The Hawk's Nest Incident: America's Worst Industrial Disaster.* 1986.

Corbin, David Alan. *Life, Work, and Rebellion in the Coal Fields: The Southern West Virginia Miners, 1880-1922.* 1981.

Erikson, Kai T. *Everything in Its Path: Destruction of Community in the Buffalo Creek Flood.* 1976.

Giardina, Denise. *Storming Heaven.* 1987.

Lewis, Ronald and John Hennen. *West Virginia: Documents in the History of a Rural-Industrial State.* 1991.

Stutler, Boyd B. *West Virginia in the Civil War.* 1966.

Trotter, Joe William. *Coal, Class, and Color: Blacks in Southern West Virginia 1915-1932.* 1990.

Waller, Altina. *Feud: Hatfields, McCoys, and Social Change in Appalachia, 1860-1960.* 1988.

Williams, John Alexander. *West Virginia and the Captains of Industry.* 1976.

LATIN AMERICA
Research Guides:

Alexander, Robert J., ed. *Bibliographical Dictionary of Latin America and Caribbean Political Leaders.* 1988.

Collier, Simon and Thomas Skidmore, eds. *The Cambridge Encyclopedia of Latin America and the Caribbean.* 1992.

Handbook of Latin American Studies. Published Annually.

Books:

Beezley, William H. and Judith Ewell. *The Human Tradition in Latin America: The Twentieth Century.* 1987.

Bethell, Leslie, ed. *The Cambridge History of Latin America.* 6 vols. 1985.
Black, Jan Knippers, ed. *Latin America. Its Problems and Promises.* 1991.
Burkholder, Mark and L.L. Johnson. *Colonial Latin America.* 1990.
Burns, E. Bradford. *Latin America: A Concise Interpretive History.* 1990.
Bushnell, David and Neill Macauley. *The Emergence of Latin America in the Nineteenth Century.* 1988.
Keen, Benjamin. *A History of Latin America.* 2 vols. 1992.
Lockhart, James and Stuart B. Schwartz. *Early Latin America.* 1983.
Szulc, Tad. *Fidel: A Critical Portrait.* 1986.
Wright, Thomas C. *Latin America in the Era of the Cuban Revolution.* 1991.

HISTORY OF SCIENCE AND TECHNOLOGY
Research Guides:
Dictionary of Scientific Biography. 17+ vols. 1970.
ISIS Cumulative Bibliography of the History of Science. 5 vols. 1989.

Books:
Butterfield, H. *The Origins of Modern Science.* 1965.
Dales, R.C. *The Scientific Achievement of the Middle Ages.* 1973.
Farrington, B.R. *Science and Politics in the Ancient World.* 1940.
Hankins, Thomas. *Science and Enlightenment.* 1985.
Hodgson, F.R., ed. *The Place of Astronomy in the Ancient World.* 1974.
Kuhn, T.S. *The Copernican Revolution.* 1966.
Lindberg, David C. and Ronald L. Numbers, eds. *God and Nature: Historical Essays on the Encounter Between Christianity and Science.* 1986.
Lloyd, G.E.R. *Magic, Reason, and Experience: Studies in the Origin and Development of Greek Science.* 1979.

Merton, R.K. *Science, Technology and Society in Seventeenth Century England.* 1970.

Westfall, Richard. *The Construction of Modern Science.* 1971.

APPENDIX A

A FEW TYPES OF HISTORIES

For centuries political and military history dominated the study of the past. But history has divided into different and overlapping topics, particularly during the last thirty years. Here are a few:

ECONOMIC HISTORY includes economic uses of land, resources, labor, and capital, and those who influenced and carried out policy. Examples: Tudor inflation, Victorian population growth, the standard of living under industrialization.

SOCIAL HISTORY involves human relations of different classes, family and household life, conditions of labor groups and leisure time. Examples: child labor laws and the change in sexual mores in the United States after the advent of penicillin and the birth control pill.

RELIGIOUS HISTORY addresses why people follow religious practices and how churches respond to society. Examples: Gothic architecture's purposes during the Middle Ages and the impact of Islam on the Christian West.

HISTORY OF SCIENCE includes the science and technology that was part of a culture and the changes it caused. Examples: the effects of genetic engineering, steam engines, and geometry.

ART HISTORY reveals information about a culture and mirrors its surrounding society. Examples: the impact of perspective on Renaissance art and art as a propaganda tool during the French

Revolution.

INTELLECTUAL HISTORY deals with the ideas, thoughts, arguments, beliefs, assumptions, and preoccupations of people at a given time. Examples: Plato's view of the state and Descarte's scientific method.

AFRICAN-AMERICAN HISTORY includes the lives of black people who have been left out of earlier histories or whose roles are being reconsidered, particularly since the Civil Rights movement of the 1960s. Examples: the cotton gin's impact on Southern slavery and the Great Depression-era Urban League's fight for civil rights.

DIPLOMATIC HISTORY addresses relations between states, their treaties and negotiations. Examples: impact of the Washington Naval Agreement of 1922 on Japanese-American relations and the uncertain role of NATO after the Cold War.

HISTORY OF WOMEN includes still more people who have been left out of earlier histories, or reconsiders women who have been defined only in relation to the men to whom they were related. Examples: reclaiming the work of early feminists such as Christine de Pizan and Mary Wollstonecraft, and women's contributions in industry during World War II.

PUBLIC HISTORY involves studying and preserving the records of people and places and often includes positions outside academic institutions such as archives, historical societies or museums. Public History is, as it name implies, that facet of history which brings history to the public rather than keeping it in college buildings. Examples: studying land records at a courthouse or digging at a Mount Vernon excavation site.

APPENDIX B

RESEARCH GUIDES

PERIODICAL GUIDES
America: History and Life: A Guide to Periodical Literature
Historical Abstracts
Union List of Serials in Libraries of the United States and Canada
New Serial Titles: A Union List of Serials Commencing Publication after December 31, 1949
Reader's Guide to Periodical Literature

INDEXES
Biography Index: Cumulative Guide to Biographical Material in Books and Magazines
Book Review Index
Index to Book Reviews in the Humanities
Index to Women of the World from Ancient to Modern Times
Social Science and Humanities Index

DICTIONARIES AND HISTORICAL DICTIONARIES
A Dictionary of Modern History, 1789-1945
Concise Dictionary of American History
Oxford English Dictionary
Webster's New Collegiate Dictionary, 9th edition

GENERAL AND HISTORICAL ENCYCLOPEDIAS
Encyclopaedia Britannica
Encyclopedia Americana
Encyclopedia of World History, Ancient, Medieval and Modern,

Chronologically Arranged
Encyclopedia of the Social Sciences

ATLASES
Atlas of American History, 1984
The Times Atlas of the World
Atlas of World History

BIOGRAPHICAL AND OTHER GUIDES
A Bibliographic History of Blacks in America Since 1528
American Men and Women of Science
Biographical Directory of the American Congress 1776-1979
Biographical Directory of the Government of the United States
Biographical Sources for Foreign Countries
Book Review Digest
Dictionary of African Biography
Dictionary of American Biography
Encyclopedia of World Biography
Foreign Relations of the United States
Historical Statistics of the United States
History of Science and Technology: A Select Bibliography
Guide to Reference Books
International Who's Who
Library of Congress Subject Headings
National Cyclopedia of American Biography
Statistical Abstract of Latin America
Who's Who in America
Who Was Who in America
Who's Who in Latin America

NEWSPAPER DIRECTORIES
Christian Science Monitor Index
Newspapers in Microform: United States 1948-1983 (2 volumes)

New York Times Index
Official Index to the Times [of London]

GOVERNMENT PUBLICATIONS
Cumulative Subject Guide to United States Government Bibliographies, 1924-1973
Monthly Catalogue of United States Government Publications

APPENDIX C

HISTORICAL SOCIETIES AND ORGANIZATIONS
(A Partial Listing)

Directories of organizations:
Directory of Affiliated Societies (American Historical Association)
The Directory of Federal Historical Programs and Activities (Society for History in the Federal Government)
Enclyclopedia of Organizations

Organizations:
Advisory Council on Historic Preservation, 1100 Pennsylvania Ave., NW, Washington, D.C. 20004 (202-254-3967).
Air Force Historical Foundation, Building 1413, Rm 120, Stop 44, Andrews AFB, MD 20331 (301-981-4738).
American Association for State and Local History, 172 Second Ave., North, Suite 102, Nashville, TN 37201 (615-255-2971).
American Association of Museums, 1225 Eye St., NW, Suite 200, Washington, D.C. 20005 (202-289-1818).
American Historical Association, 750 N. Lake Shore Dr., Chicago, IL 60611 (312-988-5000).
American Military Institute, Office of Air Force History, HQ USAF/CVAH, Bldg 5681, Bolling AFB, D.C. 20332 (202-353-5431).
Association for Documentary Editing, c/o Elizabeth Hughes, Papers of Dwight D. Eisenhower, Department of History, Johns Hopkins University, Baltimore, MD 21218 (301-338-8363).
Association for the Bibliography of History, Department of History, Georgia State University, Atlanta, GA 30303 (404-651-2250).
Committee on History in the Classroom, Creative Textbooks, 550 N. Sheridan Square, Evanston, IL 60202.
Historians Film Committee, c/o History Faculty, New Jersey Institute

of Technology, Newark, NJ 07102 (201-596-3269).

Institute for Research in History, 1133 Broadway, New York, NY 10010 (212-691-7316).

Institute of Museum Services, 1100 Pennsylvania Ave., NW, Room 510, Washington, D.C. 20506 (202-786-0539).

National Archives and Records Administration, 8th St. and Pennsylvania Ave., NW, Washington, D.C. 20408 (202-523-3218)

National Association of Government Archives and Records Administrations, Executive Secretariat, New York State Archives, Room 10A75, Cultural Education Center, Albany, NY 12230 (518-473-8037).

National Center for the Study of History, Inc., c/o RR 1, Box 679, Cornish, ME 04020 (301-770-1174).

National Conference of State Historic Preservation Officers, Hall of the States, Suite 332, 440 North Capitol St., NW, Washington, D.C. 20001 (202-624-5465).

National Coordinating Committee for the Promotion of History, 400 A St., SE, Washington, D.C. 20003 (202-544-2422).

National Council for the Social Studies, 3501 Newark St., NW, Washington, D.C. 20016 (202-966-7840).

National Council on Public History, 403 Richards Hall, Northeastern University, Boston, MA, 02115 (617-437-2677)

National Endowment for the Humanities, 1100 Pennsylvania Ave., NW, Washington, D.C. 20506 (202-786-0438).

National Historical Publications & Records Commission, National Archives and Records Administration, 8th St. and Pennsylvania Ave., NW, Washington, D.C. 20408 (202-523-1701).

National Register of Historic Places, National Park Service, P.O. Box 37127, U.S. Department of the Interior, Washington, D.C. 20013-7127 (202-343-9536).

National Trust for Historic Preservation, 1785 Massachusetts Ave., NW, Washington, D.C. 20036 (202-673-4000).

Oral History Association, Executive Secretariat, 1093 Broxton Ave.,

#720, Los Angeles, CA 90024 (213-825-7524).

Organization of American Historians, 112 N. Bryan St., Bloomington, IN 47401 (812-335-7311).

Organization of History Teachers, c/o Earl P. Bell, President, University High School, 1362 East 59th St., Chicago, IL 60637 (312-702-0588).

Phi Alpha Theta (history honorary), 2333 Liberty St., Allentown, PA 18104 (215-433-4140).

Public Works Historical Society, 1313 E. 60th St., Chicago, IL 60637 (312-667-2200).

Society for Historical Archaeology, P.O. Box 231033, Pleasant Hill, CA 94523-1033 (508-686-4660).

Society for Historians of American Foreign Relations, Department of History, North Texas State University, Denton, TX 76203 (817-565-2288).

Society for History in the Federal Government, Box 14139, Ben Franklin Station, Washington, D.C. 20044.

Society for Industrial Archaeology, Smithsonian Institute, National Museum of American History, Room 5014, Washington, D.C. 20560 (202-357-2058).

Society for the History of Technology, Smithsonian Institution, National Museum of American History, Room 5707, Washington, D.C. 20560.

Society of American Archivists, 600 S. Federal St., Suite 504, Chicago, IL 60605 (312-922-0140).

Society of Architectural Historians, 1232 Pine St., Philadelphia, PA 19107 (215-735-0224).

Western History Association, Department of History, University of Nevada, Reno NV 89557 (702-784-6852).

From *Careers for Students of History* by Barbara J. Howe (Washington: American Historical Association, 1989), 80-86.

INDEX

Academic Index, 29
America: History and Life, 40
American Historical Association, 20
Arawaks, 4
Author card, 28, 35, 36, 37, 43
Bibliographic entry, 36, 50
Bibliography, 64, 65-66, 71
Biographical Sources for Foreign Countries, 29
Body of paper, 36, 57, 58, 59-60, 65, 70
Book Review Digest, 29
Booth, John Wilkes, 10
Bound serials, 41
Boydston, Jeanne, 35, 36
Boyer, Ernest, 15, 16
Broad heading, index card, 49-50
Call numbers, 28, 37-38, 41
Card catalog, 27, 28, 30-36, 43, 44
Careers, 19-21
Carr, E.H., 14-15, 18
Catalog of the United States Government Publications, 44
Chiang Kai Shek, 17
Chicago Manual of Style for Authors, Editors, and Copywriters, 63-64
Churchill, Winston, 2
Citations, 64
Clark, George Kitson, 11
Columbus, Christopher, 3-6
Conclusion, 57-58, 70
Cortés, Hernando, 6

Coucy, Enguerrand de, 2
Cronkite, Walter, 9
Cumulative Subject Index to the Monthly Catalog of the United States Government Publications, 44
Current periodicals room, 41
Darwin, Charles, 8, 18
Databases, 29
Dewey Decimal System, 28
Dictionary, 57, 71
Dictionary of American Biography, 29
Direct Quote, 50, 62, 66
Egyptians, 10
Encyclopedia of the Social Sciences, 38
Endnote, 38, 64-65, 71
ERIC, 29
Essay, 47, 58, 68, 69-70
Facts, 1-2, 3, 4, 6, 7, 10, 11, 12, 13, 14, 18, 19, 48, 49, 50, 51, 52, 58, 62, 63, 70
Fill-in-the-blanks, 71
First draft, 66-67
Footnote, 36, 38, 39, 43, 50, 60-65, 66, 71
Footnote research, 38
Ford, Paul Leicester, 4
Foreign Affairs, 40
Frank, Reuven, 8
Froissart, Jean, 2
Galileo, 14
Germany, 6, 12, 32-34, 40-41, 45
Germany, subject heading, 32-34
Good writing, 46, 47, 60-61

Gould, Stephen Jay, 14
Government Printing Office, 44
Guide to Reference Books, 45
The Harbrace College Handbook, 63
Hispanic American Historical Review, 40
Historical Abstracts, 40, 42
Historical indices, 40-42
History Today, 40
Hitler, Adolf, 12, 13, 31, 32, 41
Howe, Barbara J., 21
Humanism, 16
Humanista, 15
Identifications, 70-71
Image History, 10
Index, 28-29, 35, 36, 40-42, 44, 45
Index card, 49-50, 51, 52, 53, 57, 64
    Broad heading, 49-50
    Source, 49
    Specific fact, 49-50
Index to Book Reviews in the Humanities, 29
Indices, 28, 39, 40-42, 44, 48
International Standard Book Number (ISBN), 36
Interpretation, 2-6, 7, 10, 11, 52, 64
Introduction, 36, 48, 57-59, 70
ISBN, 35, 36
Journal of American History, 39
Journal of Modern History, 40
Kelley, Mary, 35, 36
Kipling, Rudyard, 9-10
Labor History, 40
Leads, 50
Leutz, Emanuel, 10-11
Liberal Arts education, 15-21

Librarian, 27, 28, 29, 30, 36, 37, 42, 43, 45
Library of Congress Classification System, 28, 37
Library of Congress Subject Headings, 32-34
Lincoln, Abraham, 10
London Times, 29, 42
Manual for Writers of Term Papers, Theses, and Dissertations, 63
Manual of style, 57, 63-64, 71
Margolis, Anne Throne, 35, 36
Marx, Karl, 6-7
Matching, 71
McCarthy, Joseph, 17-18
"Meta-verdict," 8-9
Microfiche, 43
Microfilm, 43
Microform, 43
Microform readers, 43
MLA Handbook for Writers of Research Papers, 63, 65
Modern History Abstracts, 1450-1914, 40
Morison, Samuel Eliot, 3
Multiple choice, 71
National Socialism, 31-33
Nazi, 30, 31, 32, 33, 34, 40
New York Times, 28, 42
New York Times Index, 29, 42
Notes in class, 68, 69
Note-taking, 41, 46, 47, 48-52, 69, 71
Official Index to the Times, 29, 42
Outline, 53-57, 58, 69, 70
Paraphrase, 62-63
Past and Present, 39
Peloponnesian War, 2, 13

Philosophy of history, 6-8
Plagiarism, 62-63
Pokovsky, Mikhail, 16
Political Science Quarterly, 40
Pre-Columbian populations, 5
Primary sources, 342, 43-44, 48
Proofreading, 67
Pyramids, 10
Reader's Guide to Periodical Literature, 28
Reference librarian, 27, 28, 29, 30, 42, 46
Reference room, 27-30, 37, 45
Regional depository system, 44
Research notes, 48-51, 69
Rules for good writing, 60-61
Santayana, George, 13
Secondary sources, 42, 43
Serials, 41
Slavic Review, 40
Short answer, 70-71
Social sciences, 18-19, 29, 37, 38
Sources, 1, 10, 11, 12, 27, 30, 35, 39, 40, 42, 43-44, 45, 48, 49, 50, 52, 62, 63, 64, 65, 66, 71
   Sources, primary, 42, 43-44, 48
   Sources, secondary, 42, 43
Specific fact, 50
Specific fact, index card, 50
Stacks, 38, 41
Stalin, Joseph, 16
Studia humanitatis, 15
Subject card, 36
Subjectivity, 12-13
Superintendent of Documents classification, 45
Television, 8-10

Test questions, 68-71
   Essay, 68, 69-70
   Fill-in-the-blanks, 71
   Identifications, 70-71
   Matching, 71
   Multiple choice, 71
   Short answer, 70-71
   True-false, 71
Tet, 8-9
Thesaurus, 57, 71
Thesis statement, 52-53, 54, 55, 57
The Times of London, 28, 42
Thucydides, 2, 13
Title, 28, 34, 35, 36, 37, 66-67
Title card, 28, 36
Tracings, 37, 43
Transitions, 60, 67
Trevelyan, George Macauley, 8
True-false, 71
Tuchman, Barbara, 2
Turabian, Kate L., 63
Twentieth Century Abstracts, 40-41
Unbound serials, 41
Union List of Serials, 41
Vietnam, 8-9, 13, 17
Washington, George, 11
White, Theodore, 2
Wilentz, Sean, 10
William the Conqueror, 10
Wills, Garry, 5
Women's Rights, 30, 31, 35, 37, 49, 51, 63
World War II, 30, 34, 40